If It Were

... poems of the tenfolds
Joe Donald Johnson

If It Were

poems of the tenfolds

Contents

It might occur to an old poet to gather his poems.
They lay in disuse and dust-used through decades,
"the tenfolds." But might a couple of them ring still?
And it might occur to an old poet to attempt the new.
How might that go ... stumblingly? Asshpleww?

Or, out of the tenfolds in the brainfolds of the oddsockets
of the old gray pockets, might new wuh-wurds appear? You
wordsmiths will be unruffled. You third Smiths? You decide.

With reference to the numerous "peeple poems" herein:

Any resemblance to any personage,
to his betterment or worsenage,
is also resembled by that personage,
to its betterment or worsenage.

The Rock-Lake Dance

At Seeing Eye Lake there is a rock,
half the height of a man.
It circles the lake like a hand on a clock.
The photographs prove it,
a hundred and thirty years of them,
how it moves itself
lake-circle, lake-circle,
water and rock,
clock and rock,
rock and water.
Earth, quartz, crystal, gurgle.
And Seeing Eye Lake is an urgle
of ogle,
of clarity, snowmelt airity,
an eye of purity
beholding the light, the peaks, the firs,
the very stars.

The Coin in the Mitten

There was once a coin in the mitten.
Now there is paper signed and hidden.
Now there is a portfolio,
twisting like Fort Polio,
itching and intermittent.
But thanks be to the ache in life,
still there is a loin safe or smitten,
but living and not eaten.
Now there is cryptocurrency
and a hidden urgency
in the crawling numbers,
bitcoin, itcoin, a knit loining the brow.
We would hide from it
if we knew how.

Conflict

Conflict is tiptoeing, tiptoeing,
tipped are the toes.
And crippled is what conflict knows.
Quiet of toe, yet conflict claps its hands.
War in other lands
is what conflict understands.
Conflict is tiptoeing, tiptoeing,
outwitting tip the toes.
Crippled is what conflict knows.

Survive

May we survive the torrent
of twisted snarls
from on high lowly,
appallingly unregal,
twisted and twisting, all insistent,
listing toward going under.
The awful chant of the abhorrent.
A cheep in the key of awf.
A lullaby in the sigh and key of null.
In the key of nil.
May we survive the new conformant.
Children, take stealth against the informant;
he has found a new truth: the lie.
Resist, call a sister.
Untwist the speech,
word before word
after word each.
Prepare the search warrant.
Children, you are inherently unhorrid.
Fare well now.
Surveille. Pad upon paws.
Take caution of cause now.
Survive the torrent.

August 9, 2017

If It Were

We could behold a tree in the world,
a smile, a kiss,
a river empearled,
a sunset,
a dawn,
a youngling life
the earth upon,
a hope, a dream,
a magic of hand,
an absence of sorrow,
if they were,
were nothing amiss.
It could become known in us, we're
intended toward
a winded step forward,
an ongoing, a tomorrow,
if it were.

Mountain Shadow

The shades embrace our mountainsides,
then slide ... down, across, up, away.
They are little nights
walking our daytimes,
waltzing our lights,
but soundless, groundless,
mounds of umbra to the eye.
Their waltz is of the earth,
in slow earth time,
the ear can hear
if the earth heart is near.

Slopes

Here there are inclines,
slants and cants and ramps
of mountain nature, and the upping green tines
of trees, and waters dancing down gravity
from water-above places, lakes and springs.
Around the steepnesses are the places of camps.
And in the pellucid dark times
the blinking lamps
of the stars. And Time's creature,
hushed, hungry, unemerging,
familiar with upcurvatures,
lurks the margins.

Furtherance

The sun may rise tomorrow
adrip in nuclear fire.
Far away in its cosmic ire.
Only warm here.
A warmth wanting hope.
Perhaps a human will step forward,
a furtive little furtherance
of a right thing,
a dream step,
a freedom,
a love,
a belief
in bloom,
a clef of tune,
a tithing
for hunger relief,
a dressing on a wound.
So very many wounds.

A Seclusion in The Six Hills

There are citizens in a realm of six hills
who whisper among themselves.
Their concern is a burning thing.
Their yearning is an urgent thing.
But their ranks are tranquil.
Their learning discerns a disturbance in the peace
yet again, far off, behind a smoky curtain,
in a place of swarms where danger lurks.
Now in the ranging darks
an unheralded peril comes.
Somewhere in the swirling murks
there is no ought to,
but a toss fro, a crossbow staccato
salvo of the drums.

August 15, 2017

A Simple Sense

Among the flowers there is an incense,
a perception of events
occurring on the plane of subquintessence,
in an unnoticed sphere
sans pretense,
in a kind of ummmwhere,
remarkable but unremarked upon.
Above, among the stones,
there is a silent occasion
of unseen creeping occurrence,
not obvious to the eye,
oblivious to the ear,
a silent moan among the stones.
Or is it a song? some songalong, an unhearable rockaby
in the hard community of alones?
At the pond's edge
is a simple complex water fledge,
it edges understanding
with sand, with fond and tiny water dancing,
some kind of planning,
some incline of thanking.

She Nods her Head

She speaks into the phone, listens, nods her head.
They have laughed at those who nod on the phone,
who shake their heads.
The laughers may own their opinions.
But she knows, without wonder,
in the gentle wind around the payphone,
there is someone there.

Buzzard Circle over Etna

Over Etna the buzzards are circling on motionless wings,
the circle moves to the north, a wing of command flaps,
the circle moves south.
Below lies death or near-death, and high into the sky
in the sun's lit weather,
in the sussing air of the feather,
in the bird wind
it is known, buzzardblack on blue.

Barcelona Now

A van. A man.
Another man.
A woman.
A child.
Speed.
Horror.
Death. Injury.
Barcelona.
The unthinking and unseeing
are saying they did it.
The Blissless Archaic Bygone Goneby Agonistic State
is saying their soldiers did it did it.
They did it, did it, in spite of a world of knowing.
In spite of understanding
aglow in all directions.
In spite of mother and daughter and stepson and lesson.
In spite of the whirling caresses of caring.
In spite of a future.
In spite of nurture.
In spite of all.

August 17, 2017

A New Conversation

Newly, conversations flit
from idea to hit.
Where went the true exchange of thought,
the forming-up of the idea
from within, three a
moment, a reason within dialog?
A bridge across minds.
Where went the listen?
We have here the fleet speech parchment of the time.
The mind lunges. It lurches.
It goes.
On the parchment, quickenscratches,
pigeon itchings,
erasures and didn'ts,
the barren leavings of the unsaid.

Eclipse

There is a shadow upon the dayworld
creeping across the orb.
There is a confusion of shades
acreep and new and inching toward blue
across our glades.
Ask any herb.
There is a dayworld falling asleep.
Its purpose, its winnows, its doings, its cause.
All lapsing and nodding off.
A shadow coming, a shadow unknowing,
acreep and new and inching deep blue.
What to think true.
How to peer through.
How to know now
what once you knew.
What to do.

August 21, 2017

Concern

Concern is lurking
birdlike and fluttering,
over the lectern,
in the butter churn.
In the meeting adjourned,
see the lips turning.
Soundless are the lips.
Yet someone does an about turn.
Did you say that?
Are we warned?

Upstart Crow

The crow with a speech of screeches
uplifts, upwings, uprises,
utter flutter, for up is up.
Brief I beheld his knowing eye. It spoke:
"My play is finished.
The Crow King Oakmount the One-hundred-thirty-third
in the Land of the Croaks."
In the land of oaks.
The upstart is beautified with our feathers.
Never doubt it.
Never doubt its parliaments.
Never doubt its knowing,
its picking of locks
and lifting of levers,
its pecking at plays,
its treelimb dancing,
its measuring of the whethers.

Yosemite 1851

Ahwaneechees were they.
Pale of face were the newcomer others.
And in all they were few
and they were brothers
but thought not of it,
not one, not another.
What were the wars for? the bursts of brainrage
among the sugared pines
and into the snowload sequoias,
splashing the clean creeks
under the marble monoliths,
the gunning contested suns
and the guarded deadlocked nocturnes?
the dying cry from the living lip?
Trees, whose rivers were these? shadows, whose meadows?
The host Yosemite soars mighty, Ghost Enmity, your cemetery.

Markroy Coddleston

A rotund bundle of fifty-six years
and less than five feet tall
who may be seen
huddling to leeward
of a rack of newspapers
every windy day
in old san jose
and never when the sun shines
and it's warm,
only in the cold
and the wind.
He is toothless
and calls the headlines out
like lamenting the dead.
Hence "Barkboy the Newser."
Ask if he's well
and you get one line.
"You'll never know the news I've had."
Never when the sun shines
and it's warm,
only in the cold
and the wind.

Lafwerk

A Dutch ancestry and a windmill name,
he claimed. And since he could laugh
like Thunder's wondrous rolling of the drums,
that laugh drew attention some.
And since he carried within him
an elemental dissatisfaction
with work and other sorry states
of employment and unjoyous transaction
you know what they tagged him.
Laughwork.
But they didn't hang that on him
because he laughed at work.
He earned that label by laughing at labor
and other sad states of employment and transaction
so loudly and so long and so gladly in song
and with such exertion of abdomen and countenance
that his laughing was work.
And after a year or four and four more
of genuine enterprising
extensive physiognomizing,
he developed a means of solid subsistence
exclusive of work and other sick incidents
of employment and arrangement and transaction,
based on his unmistaken premise
the world would pay to see him grimace
pure and pristine and unpatented.
Which set him free to laugh for bread.

Lazarus Leppernatch

Lazarus if you had met him
would have told you
that he hated his name.
People met him and uttered "Behold you"
before he could mutter "Hello, you."
But now that you mention it
he did feel a mite lethargic.
But no one ever called him forth, that he knew of,
and he counted on what he knew.
Not that he disbelieved, you see,
only that belief came about more easily
when he touched on evidence
or beheld with his own torches.
And yet there is something important behind our porchlights.
An overarching thing, a mind, a spirit rise.
And because that is so, you had to admit
if you really thought down and added it
that just about anything is possible.
And a need can be great—
so you would never find him critical
or even a little whippoorwillical
of anything you believed or needed.

Holloran

out of Natchez
in a big wind and a rain
northward
for peace
of mind or spirit.
He fled the rain until he couldn't feel it,
the wind until he couldn't hear it.
He was one of a kind in Natchez.
He was matchless out of Natchez.
Near Topeka the owner of a diner
asked Holloran, "Where you bound?"
Holloran replied, "Been one where, been another where.
Long's I get there or go there, don't really care.
I think the thing I'm seeking can be found."
But at the door he paused and turned back.
"Truly," he said, "where I'm bound
is a goodly question.
I suppose I intend to learn some lesson.
I could answer 'North.'
Or I could answer 'Away from where I've been.'
Or I could answer 'Where we all are bound,
you and I and the fox in the hole.'
Or I could answer 'To a place where I cannot but be.'
North to the caribou or thereabouts.
But truly, sir, truly, I'm not sure
whether I want the getting there
or the I'm-gone going."

Misogynist

A devout
hater of women
(self-announced)
holding the plight
of the populous earth
high for an omen,
runs out
shouting loud
denouncements
of lust and birth,
as certain as he is sad
that all the mad
mislaid misled
mistaken tomorrows
were the sorrows
of love (all was futility),
knowing but to fault
the fertility of the seed
for the burning bough
that burns in need.

The Nasty Urchin

O emplanted nasturtium,
up from your earthium
when?
when?

Belief

To hold a belief is a simple matter.
One's psyche clings.
A simple thing.
Why, though?
To what?
And this: Why, from a held belief,
from wall, from sconce,
from candle, from once,
would one turn suddenly away,
toward the moon's face,
toward a star place,
toward a place of aways
and unvisiteds?

or, one who opposed violence with violence
because violence refused to listen to peace.
But the violence ate at the cause in his heart,
defied and denied its lovely purpose,
fire laughing at water,
a meteor disdaining Space.
Then in the conflagracelessness of social agitation
his arm snapped in a midthrow hasten,
his stride broke on the brick he dropped,
and hard did he find the pavement.
From a mere nearness of twenty strides
he saw among runners Death politely strolling,
Death who should have been
a brawny fencebuilder
and a spader of earth,
a flaring dragon, unseemly demon,
Death serenely strolling in a half-war,
an unheeded prophet in a white loincloth
who had been fair in prophecy always,
and warned against himself,
and never smiled with the taste of new conversions.
Then the eyes of that wizened prophet
fell calm on the eyes of Rebexus Reed.
Those pundit lips of suspended Life
parted to speak this sentence,
or was it to ask this question:
"I see into your heart.
Loving me and hating me,
why are you not one?"

Werdsferth and Gyner

Werdsferth carries
a righthandless, leftlegless Gyner
down the finewind dunes of shipshod beach
daily, morning and evening each.
Every nine steps
they fall down laughing,
two inepts ...
or Werdsferth drops Gyner
and they are four lips laughing,
the friend no finer
and the jettisoned recliner.
Where is there to go but laughter?
Superbly are they absurd,
these two unmadeup clowns.
They fall again on sandy downs.
It seems to be an awkward labor,
carrying a man who lacks a leg and a gripper:
you don't quite remember
which member to grab for.
Or which dismember was left behind
on a war's abhorrent floor.
It is riding Gyner on Werdsferth's back
but I wonder who is carrying whom.
One of them arises
laughing from the sand
and suddenly sees the day ahead
in the same different land
when he will come laughless
down the finewind dunes
without that blessed burden,
the laughing backpack lacking—
alone, alone, a duo of one
down the finewind dunes
of shipshod beach.

Lewie

Lewie has a right to his laggard constitutionals
down the corridors of his institution
muttering, mumbling, mumming to himself.
He's seen a little, a liter, a loaf, a fatherlode
of life his ninety winters.
Imagine, can you, all of that pleasantness.
Can you tally that many smiles, so many?
Here is his twillionth— instant bliss, then isn'tness.
Can you heft the awful anvil
where the anguishes were struck?
Lewie has a right to his tardy constitutionals
through the horror doors, down the corregidors of his institution.
The pages of rage are burned away,
there's a trace crust of char
edging his eyes where the wrinkles are.
Now try, can you, to forget a week, forget a month
of the faces in his faded far.
They ebbed into never
like snowflakes aflown,
like the mating of mollusks,
like tempests emptied
in their infant sea.

Soyo

Soyo wanders the corridors
of a state hospital
in California,
mental place, mad place, demented.
Soyo wanders
nor over, nor under,
but corridor door
to corridor door.
I must want in vain to tell you
of a certain
wistful windblown look
around his eyes.

Dunn

Mr. Dunn wants peace.
In his uneven evenings drones a dirgeful din.
Mr. Dunn prays peace. War is not Dunn.
Dunn's deeps are sleepless; his dreams bleed screams.
The night alights, sleep creeps, the X-loads explode,
the permissible little missiles
just miss.
Dunn's dark is Parkinsonian, his tremblers remember,
his clubbed members tremor,
he's a palsy under a pall,
a soul in chorea.
Father Life, Mother Love,
S.O.S., can you save Dunn,
the horror-hounded fox in the bloody burrow
shuddering his thunder in,
awaiting the snowflake enemy enigma,
the blizzard wizards, the ice men
who cometh, who gunneth
ever, forever his feared, feared fire?

Enduro Henry Durendy

We are born into a test of our endurance—
a year-after-yearathon
of how we wear them,
how we bear the bearing,
how we stand before the tempest,
how tenaciously we cling
whilst the demons pull.

I inform you that Henry Durendy did cling—
in the womb,
at the breast,
to the textbook,
in the foxhole,
in the hospital,
at the workplace,
to the home,
to the family members
dying like predawn embers
of accident, malice and malady,
Henry Durendy did cling fast against
the persistent lombardment
of the farces existent ...

Time erodes being.
Time eroded all that Henry Durendy
cherished. The passion that cherishes
wills the cherished endlessly unperished.
Cannot be. All things being endy.

But there was a miracle
around Enduro Henry.
The miracle around him was
that heart-mummed, stone-stunned,
his mind of no inkling,
he by somehows crept on with going,

one step, another step, through the coals lost glowing,
he succeeded in proceeding,
doing as he could for what was showing,
what was needing.

Wherefore herewith sincerely and now
I do salute him. To Enduro Henry
(and those in his image).
To his life, to his effort, to his intrepid trudge.
He was indeed a tenacious clingling,
for he onward and he onward went ...

this path of passage and of wonderment.

Nassio

There are spent ones who drop out.
For their opting out,
some poet will wonder on them.
And ponder their anthem.

Take Nassio.
An erstwhile technical specialist
in neo-franchisable subcrystalline frigiphysics

he, whom I meet now in his neo-independence
on Sagebrush Drag in Ghostpost, Nevada
(an erstyear worstwhere goner of a place),

he's crouched in a longevous crossleg squat
as if for a certain coming closer yet
to a true new moon of thought.

He smiles. "Hello and hello again.
The second hello is for all the times
I might have said it but didn't

"as first I served the need that
beat at my selfness, and I fed it.
But one's soul is a river and trans-astral space."

Hup-Two

Uptown is the memory of someone's
once imprisoned father
chevroned as time's candy cane,
a memory you will never notice,
skulking innocuously pedestrious
down first street among the rest of us
in the form of that father's
fifty-year-old son, Hup-Two,
at liberty yet similarly sequestered,
upon whose chest the shadows of the bars
meet welded yet at evening,
and who still is small enough
to escape between a pair of them
to honor properly his father's earthen mask
by pilfering your silver slivers,
a surly and unbrethrenly task.

Impression of Hotflagon Fluggrey

He rises early in the morning
just to walk around all day and guzzle
in the flagon.
His problem—ask him—is
as contemporary as a pistol's muzzle.
Drunkenness is abreast
of the times, a true test
of the current moment.
There is nothing recent or unique
about a bottle, but it is exactly
and matter-of-factly
up to the instant,
as advanced as the modern day,
you might say.
But it is also an omen.
No worry of his, not his bother:
others will drive away
the long black eventual
wagon.

Black Kettle

There would have been peace, Motavato,
had the ripple from your fingers in the water
splayed on any human shore.
For you had the motive about you.

As long as your people were gathered with you
one huddled mass
under the bestarred banner of the United States of America
and the true white flag of truce
no soldier would fire upon you,
was it not to be so?
But at Sand Creek, dreamful drummers, the oncomers were demons
of one steel resolve: to wade in gore,
to harvest scalps, to slaughter, to dechild,
to perpetrate their pitiless posthumous surgeries.
Present or absent the warrior and the war.
Truly, truly, was it not so?

Not born with two hearts ... the one you had
was heart enough for two.
                                        On Washita River, in yet another of life's
            camps,
once again you would have made peace,
you were possessed of the words and the will to speak them;
but grim Dastard Pilgrim Death
from out of the four winds came at a gallop,
they tell of it, in the quiet snow came riding,
Custer, Garry Owen, Jones and Elliott and Smith and Mayhem.
For your hand in peace and your one heart
your greeting hailed the dyingball, the bullets screaming,
and you, "old cypher," your wife, your people,
toppling aside before the white stampede.

Peace. Peace was proclaimed by the muzzle from the east.
The gun has set.

We go no more among the glowing knolls
eyes asearch upon the fired horizon.
Buffalo. Pony heard. Arapaho. No.

The long breath that truly
truly is the wind ... we hear it.
And in the water, cycled again and still again
from Sand Creek and the Washita River
through the great clouds, through the rains and snows,
in the water the ripplets
dispatched of no fingers
emanate yet, now if not forevermore
splaying out their landfall on a shore despirited.

There You and I Go

There you and I go
A million separate ways
For thirty thousand days
And what to show?

There you and I climb
A myriad unrelated hills
Under two divergent wills
And that is what became of time.

Clemsoe, Machinist

and mechanic.
Clemsoe knows machines of an infinite variety,
manufactures them
maintains them
repairs them
invents them.
He is one with machines.
His hands, in fact, are machines.
And he believes a machine
pumps infallibly
in the heart of darkness.

The Man(like)

There is a man(like)
never had a name.
He softly treads an island forest
and a highland granite.
He speaks an airless silence.
He has a brother, bald, running counter, and far off,
where the trouble rises,
where the angers blare.
Where never the head congratulates the hair.
The man(like) quietly pads the forest of the spirit
and knows his own shadow and can hear it,
but fears the shadow of his frowning counterpart
and fears the beating of that counter heart.
The man(like) will leave his counterpart
to counterpartake until he languishes,
to crush what he will crush and to be what he is:
pillager of hopes, attender to anguishes.

Wolcott Emery

A brief poetic Wolcott Emery:
Wolcott Emery, who would have employed
his life, his energy, his entity's entirety
in the endeavor of the betterment
of the human and earthly environment,
neither of which would have aught to do
with Wolcott's motives, which they could hear no throat of,
and with which they were pre-abruptly done.
Didn't they know him—Wolcott the One?
His second coming was less joyed
than the first—humanity was in fetters:
bureaucracy, militia, nation, slumber, letters
aflame, deconstructure, precedent, creed.
His fourth forthcoming fell more futile
than his third. Stasis was an army of ghosts in a bastion
of centuries.
        So here is your question:
Why would human man and fuming earth
not welcome with open hearts and lands
his true embodiment of behoovement
when it came ringing at the mundane gate,
free of charge, devoid of guile,
writing its book, singing,
living for liberation,
vying for vaccines,
plying for ploughshares,
trying for treaties?
So, so, with time evanescent
his Emeryesque energy and his sunlit summons
went waning, waning,
man and earth went wanting, did they not,
                do they not?
And of our forthcomer, what, what?
Wolcott? Wolcott?
All out of time.
Out of all memory.

At the Memorial to Dr. John Fife,
Red Bluff, California, July 7, 1971

Fifty-two years is not a long time to live.
Children run the turf at fullmoon dusk
calling Uncle John,
who is perhaps sixty, perhaps seventy.
How long will the full moon take
to become the sun all abake?
Night will be forgotten then.
In fifty-two years
a man might never upon a sunrise
set unhurried eyes.
And it is far easier to live
than to give.
And easier to live
than to trust
in the giving.
In fifty-two years
a man might seldom
take a deep breath, apart from the bedlams.
Yet for this man's fifty-two
he is called beloved,
and from the stone
given to his memory
the thirst of his brothers
and his brothers' sons
forgets itself this day,
for they are not alone.

The Bamboo Curtain

Across the clear gray shroud
of our madeup American mind
the baldfaced someones of public influence
have drawn a twisted line in Red ink
over which wellwish is treasonous to step.
While the someones powerful
in the Wargames Room, in the Itchy Nation Room,
grimmed laborious over the curvature
of that serpent on the map
of a world urgent and nervous sure,
the old faraway monsoon rattled baptismal
on the broadleaves and the thatched hamlet huts.
But the clean green jungle never spoke a syllable
nor felled the brazen bamboo of its flesh
to add yet another division to the planet.
The someones powerful
knived the paper planet's body,
called the writhing Red result a curtain
and called it closed.
Wellwish is treasonous to step over.
Is it against all the neutral silence of the jungle
and in view of all the humanoid sentries
that cobras are said to guard the mind?

—*1970s. A war troubled my people.*

A Result and Anthrus Boyd

An invention
and a solution
and a result
lay dying
in a sewage drain that muttered
nothing newage.
The nearest anthropoid,
Anthrus Boyd,
a solid citizen
and a lofty intention
given to many pauses,
was all for sanctifying
flags and institutions
with a plenty and a twenty of restitution.
Fervent liberations
and other great causes,
oh so subject to his pauses,
could wait until his bread was all unbuttered.

A JB Apparition

A strange strange bearded man I should say of him,
he leapt at me out of the night.
"Do you know me?" he asked.
"Many people know me still.
They've written poems and songs about me
and men like me,
about the error that I made
in my campaign to liberate mankind,
how the majors conferred and ruled I would die
because no state of war existed,
while they filed their birthstones into bullets
at the smoking compass points.
Are you aware as many are
of a certain piety and nobility I had?
And many refer to the whiskey of cause
I drank into drunkenness.
Then I stumbled unarmed from armaments,
walked up secure in motive,
invulnerable in ideal, and died.
Do you know me?
A few have even claimed to know
of that liberated multitude
I beheld in passing:
all the dancing hues of execution."

At This Place

The winds lash the countenance
of the custody of man
at this place to which I have been driven.
A boy screams out, he would burst his lungs,
against his perception
time elapses.
He is fifteen years old.
And they will seclude him like a shrine
in a room narrower than the mind.
And the long arms of umbrage
will pummel the many-eyed faces of buildings,
at this place. I have been driven.

The Rib

I work in a sighlum.
Parr, one of my paranoids,
has this skit of frenzied forensics:
he rants in group therapy every Thursday
the battle of the sexes is a new clear war
puffing powder this very minute,
full of semen and complexes,
this is the worst day yet,
men must win it,
women desert you.
Women serve you just your desserts.
Parr's raving. He is Parramanic. It's paranoise, Parr's noise.
I want to tell him to take what he can get,
sign for his parcel
and thank his half moons,
but he can't get it.
He wants his rib back.
There's the rub.
He wants her rib.
What is all this wrap around woman's rib?
Do we doll her in ribbin's?
Have we her in our cage?
I tell Parr to count his ribs.
He counts to twenty-three.
I tell him she didn't get her ribs that way.

I pass Delilah in the aisle.
She is delighted, she kisses, I scent Delilacs.
And I sense, within her form I love,
that stands without me,
the curved milk bone.
I have here another,
if she happens that way.

—*1970s*

They Call Him "Legs Alone"

He dreams of publishing his legs.
He can tell you all about
what the city looks like
from four inches above the sidewalk.
He has a little board on wheels
bestowing upon him the mobility
of an eel.
It beats a hidewalk.
Few can claim to know the city
with quite his perspicacity.
From a legless rollingboard
you see the undersides of people,
as it were,
a constant abscondering yonder,
the unwondering bottomside of the mind,
the white writhing
mass foot-and-kneeing underbelly
of mankind.

He smiles up at just about anyone
and says he will rise up yet.
"Do you know how?
It's the book I'm writing.
All about everything I never did
with those two legs I lost."
Then he adds, "Have peace."

You Have No Faith in God, You Say

because God, being nonexistent, has none in you.
Talk. You have an hour. I will be your disciple,
one megaphonic ear and mindful.
Tell me what you know.
But teacher, tell me also
how you've come to know it.
Pregenesis was so long ago—
a Dusting cloistered by the Darkness.

I will listen, then in doubt, no doubt,
within and throughout,
go my uncertain way about,
and down the path of questions.

I've spoken with your antithesists.
They are injected with awesome antidotes
to the clockknot logic of whyologists.
Wearers of the many coats
of one belief ... but are they armied marionettes,
inspired scions of the Righteous Icon
but not of the Master Void, not of Allness?
Not of an Unknowable Mind beyond Darkness and Time.

But my home is now a nihilist's billet
and I an hour am your disciple
as nigh as I can will it.
Tell me, has It a nothing form,
a nil eternal, neverlasting, evernot,
has What a visage of abysses,
is He a firmament of frothing tombs,
She a lunaverse of cold cocoons?

— probably 1970s; 2017

Abigail Abbins

female test pilot
who dared to fly and who flew,
who finally climbed down
and cried
but said she had learned something
up there amid the blue.
That for the guiding power in your life
you had to rely on you
and on that which was not you.
In a vastness of sky
you had to rely
on some mysterious mission beyond yourself,
beyond the peering of your eye,
and hope for a pittance of control.
When asked for advice she ponders,
then shrugs like a rug and laughs:
Grab the helm and love the storm.

The Ghost Hospital

Perhaps they have condemned
this hollow hulk.
Once it was a building-wrap
for the human.
Now it is a sallow sulk.
Now, though absent the "This Building Condemned" signs,
it cannot but be condemned, knows the mind.
It groans with the sounds of years ago,
agonies come and gone.
Becalmed, it moans with wind.
It fills with shadows
at high noon, afternoon, moon swoon,
all the same.
Among the other harmed chateaus
it weeps its dire escrow,
groans its olden doings so,
crestfalling, on a going bias, dyingmost.

Foxborne's Knocks

Foxborne sustained himself on beaver
from year 'forty-four
to year 'forty-severe
and finally found the diet
upheave-oh and irreverent;
and demented, he meant it.
Whereupon he went over to fox
for another year or three
but found it sincerely
similitudinous to beaver
(even married with berries
and furbished with phlox).
Whereupon he went over to love
and found the sustenance he was seeker of;
but after fifty years of hers,
they loving him and he them,
he swore it was the spiritual equivalent
of fox and flocks and beaver,
nothing more by damn.

Night Lights

The lucencies dance across the night,
leaping, migrating, porch, mall, torch,
auto in lurch.
Candle in church.
Lightwalk, skywalk, light following talk.
And lucents unknown,
subtleties, gluttonies, studies and cuddlings,
the eye follows, learns
but not all, discovers
but is left puzzling,
as the brightnesses
don cloak in the
dark and darkening
mysteries of nightness.

The Three Feet of Argmont

Argmont was three feet tall.
He skimbered anywhere, anywhere at all,
with no one knowing his scamper was a skimber,
a special getabout all in limber
and done with three feet
and you heard not a skitter.
Argmont had our documents,
our documents all,
scanned all our documents
and stored them in locker dents.
He never needed one, as never was he knocked against.

To Theodore Waiting

Not one more measle of an inch forward will I step,
Theodocius, until you halt that grabby lip.
The ship
is only late,
I tell you.
I think this fiend that holds you
is almost
hate—
for this you had me falling most
of the way to the harbor.
Perhaps at your last haircut that little snipposlav of a barber
neglected
to nick for once your ear.
I'm telling you Teddy we all need those heady little nicks,
they make our niches
in this world.
I've never seen you so uncollected
and so begirled
as you are here.
Lorry, Theodory, you'd think she was *beautiful*.
It's obvious she is Thee-adored.
That makes her you'd-iful.
Believe me, her boat
is better
than a storm in a moat,
makes a song
of weather.

She'll be along.
Keep it together.

The Quick Prognosis of Hosart Hoskins

Asked his opinion on the current war
Hosart sulks behind ideologies with a grin
and answers,

"You want to know what Hosart thinks?
Some kingsnurd always starts things.
I think I have peered with heartstrings
into a numbing future.
I saw a man stumbling
in a leafless landscape
in a lethal smoke
and heard him cough
and knew him broken
and saw him fall.

"I think I have peered further into the future.
I saw a land and a sky and a deluge
and no living creature.

"I think I have peered further into the future.
I saw a man walking by a river.
Strangely content he looked.
I asked him, 'Is there a war on, anywhere?'
He answered with a vague smile,
                              'Long, long ago.'"

The Green

They say Baudelaire
dyed his hair green.
I don't know that about green.

But I am witness to its daily industrees
around the latest parthenons of ministries.

They say that sorceresses
come green-eyed.
I don't know that about eyes.

But mine have visited the ministries
catacombed with corridors
grandpaternally greenless, statistically sinister,

officed with admonishing administers,
moanfully monotoned
cutlessly conknifing come-inisters;

brother, sister.

Anything-Salesman

He lights up
watching the street
mill millipedal over itself
mewling, bleating—like a mutant infant
providently blinded
to its legs too many.

Here they come again
he thinks.
They have everything
yet they come again.
What is the unpurchasable
they would purchase?
Possessing the estates that they possess
yet empty within as they are empty,
why do they not go away
from thieves and all these squealing lights
confusing their darknesses,
and live?

But O they appease my horrible hunger
coming to buy again.

Faunt Remembers

They went smiles and years
out of their way
to teach me morality
but taught me tears.
And they taught me fear.
They taught a morality
of harm, some fighting knell,
it twisted me near
to a nightspell.
Could they have intended
this frightful hell?
I am now a black cat
creeping a night fence
toward offence
and hating the little wind
that blows in me.
Now I howl in every alley
and weep without a sound
in every hospital zone.

Half Hermit Judney

At times, but only partly for a lark
Judney ghost-speaks in St. Luke Park
joining McWhenley on McWhenley's horse.
"You down there, can you hear my voice?
Step up a little closer boys
and put the bottles down.
Mindsleep follows habit, brothers.
Meaninglessness follows insignificance.
Enough of it.
Slough it off.
Come out with me.
We'll view such outcome as we can see.
We'll set a few young children free,
free in the mind.
I have a cabin over Seventeenth Ridge
but it's a place I come back to
and I don't have to have it.
The lakes are fishy and ashimmer.
The soil is ever the rich
with worms.
Sign right here if you want to be a member.
Come on your own terms,
but bring a child with you when you come,
your own child, the one forgotten.
Those of you who haven't signed,
it's almost night now
so don't decide now.
Sleep on it. Wake on it. Abide on it.
I'll ride this horse again tomorrow.
Our course is cast in cantering stone
for an endless summer gone from sorrow."

There Is O Yes

There is, O yes, a haven in darkness
where the mind, in a rude neglect
of inducements, might equal peace,
and the body step into the pace
of the stars, equal pace,
and peace be unto every agonist.

Yet they clatter off in crazèd paces.
Traffic they in armaments,
barter in estrangements.

A paint-smirched artist shall portray your faces
under the regal rift of swords
and in a fratricide of blood-laked places.
That artist is poor as a peacock.
He believes, and murmurs the words,
that wars of slime shall lime your traces.

Mind might equal peace, O yes,
in crass dispassion for tenacities.
Give the mind an hour to be late in.
Feed it the gentlest of debates.
And to the agonist in his panting mime,
painfreedom, and his eighty stars of time.

An Expendy Tour

The people will gnaw hunger in an hour.
They are on a food reconnaissance with common sense,
inspecting with peculiar preculinary power
the latest crop erosion, and the prices that mark it,
with eyes that are lit with fervor
in the frigid oven of forever.
Costs are zooming, caution the consumers.
Their cautions are pre as cautions ought to be
against this commercial immersal of our time,
which green and knotted be.
Their thrive shall be tiredly tried at all eternities,
they must cut corner, blacken market,
count caringly,
be thieving verily
the crucial crumbs off the money muffin,
a hovering huffball
coughing up everything, governing all,
yet full of nothing, puffing airily.

Newborn

Here comes another one, hopefully not
a firecracker for our big bomb.
To him or to her though, this is real news.
He wails ten pails,
Let go my leg,
Put me shut,
Where are my environmental juices?
The rudiment of expression,
the weep, the outcry, the scream
and the shriek. Rebellions
all. And all new and little
spittle-spewing hellions
phrase it. Immediately.
Except the dignified, the idle,
the quiet with horror,
the near to death, the lost,
and the late to rise.
Quick to recognize indignation,
I wish theirs a rapid appeasement.
Clap my hands.
Listen up, you infants.
Here are your new environmental juices.
This is a womb called Life,
without walls and windblown,
benighted and brilliant,
passionate and passion-cold,
rain, pain, war, hunger, loving.
All roads lead home.
Here are your orders.
Go by any route you choose.
But when you return the way you've come,
come back like a burnt match,
a figure in iced lava,
loved out and lost,
a last loch of air
in your crumbling cup.

The Sircharge

Sir V. Hamilton Reud, one of the princes,
a zooming orifice,
having campaigned complainingly
and not been rejected
the-whole-domainly,
and having therefore been elected,
is assuming office.
His first and only proclamation
deals with pecuniary wreckclamation.
There shall be a surcharge uninsteadable
upon all beverages and ginger breadables,
a yoke on all potables and edibles,
to be forked over by all foodstiffs,
no untils, no thrift, no ifs.
The greedback ocean of inflation
shall know we pour a spent libation.
So lay your sir-charged reparation
at Davy Jones's lucre and receive a paupery
of fortified enrichments.
Wealth done, one and all.
We thank you for your co-opery.

Rude Hamilton chose the surcharge
the particular vehicle of his barrage
on the pandemicity of the doughful condition
so that unsirred power may particle with partition,
so that all pay submission to Hamilton's benefition,
and Rudekind biggen with human attrition.

The Ringle Bird

In the single hamlet of Ringle
there is said to be a songbird.
It is multicolored, flutterwinged,
and all ajingle.
It visits the houses on particular limbs
of particular trees. On clotheslines in wrinkle.
It can sing the much-loved songs and jingles
of the people of the little houses of Ringle.
And it knows hymns.
The Ringlarians tell of it.
It is legend now.
We know it cannot be.

Dalmotto's Ringle

The single hamlet of Ringle
was founded by Dalmotto Ringle
who fled the king's will
in a stinging spring chill
in 1738 A.D.
He lived to be eighty.
He stayed, he
did, right where Ringle is today.
He had fled away
in his desire that rights be right
and no wrong be right
by morn or by noon or by dusk or by night.
So believed Ringle at his old campsite.

Picnic Gulp

There is a kind of peace around Picnic Gulp.
Yes, we will call it Picnic Gulp.
Folks around here can get that hungry.
Hungry enough to gulp a picnic.
Folks around here keep a fondness
for peace, ponds, picnics and bliss.
For zephyrs, sunsparkle, creeks arun,
and nothing amiss.

The Unmoderns of Calla's Hand

Calla's Hand is a smallish place
with an oldish face.
The todays of the people of Calla's Hand
are not yesterdays,
yet not quite not yesterdays,
but there are ways
to inhale a today
and exhale a yesterday.
It is about the seems, the seemlies,
the erst extremes,
the whiles of smiles,
the dalliances of dreams.

Pop Eulatius Proffit

"Old Pop Profit" went up to die
on the mountain past desire.
He blew out a breath,
lay down in a bed
of the tiniest flowers,
bedbells of the upland.
He couldn't hear them scream.
He couldn't go to sleep.
That was the first he ever knew
of his chronic insomnia.
He puffed back down the mountain
and went back to counting.
He is respectable,
but psychologically deaf and less than presentable.
He began hungry and is now obese.
He will eat you. He has such eats.
The best he knows
he cannot die,
he has insomnia,
he cannot even
slow down some era,
cannot even
see his toes, sense his woes.
Lonely is the motive
of the eating of hearts.
Pop's right hand is part bird,
he waves it away toward the mountain
he won't die on,
four or five rocks
beyond desire.

Changeling Springs

The legend says
you drink of the water there,
then you come away
but in a different air.
You know you are a changeling,
but in the water
and the mirror
and the windowpane,
and in the eyes of your friends,
no change,
no changeling.
No new arranging of things.
But you've been to Changeling Springs,
and you know.

An Army Has Invaded the Land of the Lovely

Indeed,
they've always been here.
You've met them by the hundreds.
Though they've never outnumbered
the rest of us, they're everywhere.
No count what color coats they clothe in,
black tie, brown shirt, cloak of loathing,
no matter the name of the fatherland,
their program is always the same,
pogrom, ogre ram, logjam, blog of sham.
They shall implement it with a knotted hand.
Look for renewed debates on the basic rights.
The invader will call them the basic wrongs.
You may recognize him thus.
Look for assaults upon the upholders of liberties.
Therefore, look for street warfare.
The nightlight burning of the books.
Look for five-hundred-pound explosios
lying dud for the quiet time being
in the basements of libraries—
their detonators controlled from elsewhere.
Look for centurions at the bureau of statistics,
corrupt abortings within fortress courtroom,
newly absent elders,
braintrained and believing youth,
your children enrolled in a garden unkinder;
be alert for the thought police,
dreams under martial law,
the immurement
of what is individual,
the inurement
of the sensibilities.
Learn to expect instant blindness
should you see too clearly,
paralysis

should you move circumspectly.
For this the palace of the zealous is.
And you are one potential hellion
afire in righteous resistances.
So peer into the vault of the devil, yon:
in fatal array, in countless radiant rank and stores,
the cool and constant canisters
with which the simian enemy
shall silence your unbegun rebellion.

The Rebeginning

The question: Do you know where the essence
of it went? For surely, neighbor, there were blessings.
Surely, something good at the core.
Do we turn and walk the path we traveled, walk back,
and to the beginning or near beginning go?
Or walk half there, searching for blunders?
And are we forgiving of the wrongs that show?
Surely there were blessings, neighbor.
Can we think it deeply, do we know
where the blunders roll, where the essence of it went?

The Knowing of Quaghorn Blortz

Quag Blortz is quiet in his cabin
along Nordsome Spritz.
Visit the Spritz, sometimes agush,
sometimes calmer,
Blortz will converse with you.
Strange, he can name the folks long agone,
from the days of the settlings in the settling dawn
along the Spritz.
He screeches to the peregrine,
peregrinates with the red fox.
He knows the distance to the edge
of the Asteroid Belt, the sparkling bridge
of planetoid babes.
Long, long have they swung there.
If you arrive at the Spritz wounded,
Blortz is a balmer.
You will heal of his knowing.
He knows, he says, that the Earth dreamed
as it ached in its flung becoming.
He hums the universe beginning tune
as he looks about for quartz now.
He plays an instrument he calls a Blortzhorn.
He sounds like Wagner.
"This piece is by Blortz," he will say. Then, "I knew Blortz once.
He is another Blortz now,
all full of knowing and hard to find."

The Blessed St. V. D. Dance

Friend Borntroe's ex-roommate (an All-American)
is playing a torrid game, most horrid game
of lecheration and of infestation
and when questioned he laughs his explanation,
"I have labeled my bedward boogie
'the Blessed St. V. D. Dance'

"and I am boogying because
I have scrutinized the alternative waltzes—
the listless faces of kinsmen,
the sole and only face of family,
the gabled house on Maple,
the unglad ashen-clad corporate office,
the lurching hearse of commerce,
and government, and church, and law, and cause,
and judged them lifeless"

and he boogies on
and has now forgotten everything
but the drumthrob rhythm of the hunt

although he lifts one blood-test daisy
in a memory of old poetry
and his eyes anticipate,
he plucks the first of the veins vagarious
with the sucking needle,

She rubs me,
she loves me not.

Raggedy, It Throws You

Raggarty, unemployed, unenjoyed, one annoyed,
is driving his old wood-bed truck
down the redwood park
to the quack duck pond.
He is slamming the truck door,
for all of luck is a flim and a flam
and more a deuce than a four.
Where would he go now,
this Rag, he hadn't been before?
Where did he stow the beer?
He downs can one, crushes
the can in his hand,
stares at the ducks,
zings the can their way
yelling, Here, have a bear.
He notes their quagging rushes.
Raggarty, annoyed, unemployed, a boy again,
having a day off in the park,
is chucking rocks at the quacks,
calling, Here, fowl decoy, here,
have a bite. One bite,
one mortal missile morsel,
finds its featherine bill'seye.
One quack, in the practice of madness,
storms water, calls the sun, falls
dollwinged, ductile, dumb hushed
on its pallpond, malingerer in memoriam.

—first draft 1970s; 2017

Gibson's Chase

Gibson is after a punk purloiner
who rounds the corner on a hornet wing.
Gibson, not far behind, is screaming his rejoinder
"Cease chase and face fist, thief, selfist!"
but Gibson cannot catch the twisting elf,
who makes his loop and knows every hole.
Gibson pauses at the hole
to scream in his enjoiner,
"Cease to exist or come out of there, mole!"
The monkey has swung out another hole.
A grabber baboon has Gibson's keys
and Gibson is breathing exhaustion fumes;
he halts and tries to survive being blue.
Down a furry molehole burrow
Gibson's proboscis punky has found the catacombs
not supposed to be there.
And there the punky keeps his treasure chest.
It is breathlessly still down there, and dark without moons.
Perhaps tomorrow is another day. Today,
Gibson, your galloping and crafty gibbon
shall drum his treasured chest among the tombs.

Horsecorn

Nighty is a smart horse.
His name is Nighthoof
but he prefers Nighty.
We don't know how old he is.
Decades unfolden he is.
Though he sounds like a horse, he talks to people.
He will laugh at a joke, though he laughs
like a horse in a water bucket. Hilarious.
Give him a thought absurd and ridiculous
and he sputters, the sputter sounds like "Horsecorn!"
It's his word.
He knows the difference between a thought worth a nibble
and a triffling trifle of sniffling horsecorn.
He is skeptical of eye and elliptical of mind.
Run a lap around that mind if you think you can.
Or you can stand there full of stuffing and bluffing.
Nighthoof Nighty knows whereof is horsecorn.
He hasn't lived these years for nothing.

The Boy Bobo

Up Bobby Booboo Road the boy Bobo
is pondering the wheres, whys, whiches and whatnots
of what is. What is what is? Where will what is go?
I don't know, Bobo, not to a fine droplet of knowing,
I don't.
Take a step or a bounce at a time, boy Bobo,
that is how to do it. Just keep Boboing.
You can see that far. A step. A single bounce.
Beyond is the fog of misfortune or fortune,
stones or founts,
the mist of mystery, the vague outlines,
half-doubt lines,
of tomorrow's hilltops.
Ignore the ills. See the ups.
Believe in Bobo, the man or the pup.

Bobo's Sister

Up Bobby Booboo Road the boy Bobo's sister
is little leaf-of-the-landscape Lolo.
She is everywhere.
Her mind is whispering to itself.
Telling itself what is.
There is a Lolo light
emanating from her mind,
a penumbra of unslumbering,
and there is some kind of dance
in the Lolo light, a weaving
aurora Lolo-realis,
a wonder lamp,
a shining of Lolo upon all she can see,
all she can dream,
all her believing.

A Firefight in the Civil War

The street has slept for years.
It remembers one night of braising bright
mirrored in the eyes of terror and riot
and it shall burn again tonight,
why not,
those near-same eyes feel the terror and fever again,
they are straining against their brick horizon,
peering into the smokescreen
of some powercloaked oppressor quiet and unseen.
The muscles of the street are straining
against a bleeding chain.
The aspirations of the street, canticles
of wishes, are rejecting themselves as impracticable
in the iron order of things.
The life of the street,
accustomed to dying a little in a while
like clockwork at the peacock's call,
is racing a moment, a heart confused,
toward death's embarking dark apart,
dying a modicum more,
a few dashes faster,
before it remembers the tempo and adjusts.
Though I feel no tears, with my unweeping
young ones I am weeping,
for the certain petite seedcase decedent
that shall come lying littersweet,
eyewide, unidentified,
surceased, free, late, great,
in the dawn's gray wisps of soot and fume
after the ire, the siren, the firebomb,
and the knifemissile items of progenicide
which had to be, and were, all elves aside.

— original draft 1970s; 2017

Have the Joneses Gone?

Have the Joneses gone, where, where?
Five aloneses down a thorough fear
and out of a hometown now a lair?

You might just say it was the telly that sent them,
and the words that sent them, if sent the Joneses are.

They watched as Senator Allthem Slaughter asserted
that the war was endorsed by God Almighty,
though the treaty would be signed by the sod, all cloddy.
The Joneses thought they hadn't heard it.

It seems we are pledged to overthrow regimes
of ominous socialistic confederated labor
and headed up by proletarian martyrs.
Where the Joneses came from,
enter-fearing in your neighbor's frame home
was no way at all to treat a neighbor.

Watching telly, they beheld
Dr. Ambrose Q. Amble's Amputation diet,
which, the Joneses did suppose,
was one way to lose an encounter of weight.

The watched the chief executive
vow heave-ho to hold the status quo,
the Way It Is, forever changeless.
To the Joneses and to millions that was the strangest.
The Joneses asked about opportunity for all, race relativity,
poverty, prosperity, education, the hungry, the quality
of medical heal-allity, social security, world tranquillity.
They had beheld the gulf between a mind and a muscle.

Then there was that miracle of a man,
mahatma mirror to mankind,

and mankind's image cracked malign
in the fire and whine of assassination.
Came that man's near-brother and another miracle
and that kind image fissured and shrined
in the blind fine of tax evasion.
The man hadn't known a tax from a raisin.
The Joneses were of no fine persuasion:
"You'd think to save a miracle
they'd give a tax the ax."
But that would have been empirical.

Then Mr. Friendling, Jones's boss,
passed away. Now our Jones could feel the frost.
The man who had kept
twenty-seven, and Jones,
and thrown the dogs a million bones,
was lowered away and no dog howled. Nobody wept.

Jones has veered a weird evangel and his learnèd sermon
goes like this: Merrily I wave adieu
unto you and you,
for verily the lucky sons
they are the away, the unstuckèd ones.

Where? where have the Joneses gone,
five alones down the furrow there
and out of a clone zone mortared in bone?

Esmelina's Problem

Esmelina Crittenhouse was reared on Toona Taree's
column of advice to those with needs,
so she had to believe the column, and couldn't,
and couldn't believe it, and had to,
when it was exposed to the Toona Tareelings
that Toona Taree had scalding flaws and furlongs of failings,
that she wore a satanical penile tattoo
where none but an intimate might view,
had a cellar chapel full of demons wooden,
and went home at night and washed her face in
the flushing fece basin.
The world that existed behind the world explicit
was not the world Esmelina had been facing.
What now, Esmelina, ditching it and racing?

Philo's Philosophicircuit

Philo Forlomboe had heard it said
Honesty is praised and left to starve.
Well, Greed is an omnipresent cheat preserve.
A good cheat, ah, can cheat at eighty miles per hour
if speed be.
But never fear, Truth shall conquer.
And every Truth shall yield to hunger.
Truth shall breakfast or go bonker.
And all care, careful all, says Philo.
For Greed be.

Millcorn Maddock

You know what? Maddock spent
The better part
Of all his nourishment
And all his heart
Hauling corn to the mill.
He said it was against his will.
He said it was only to make a living.
He made it with misgiving.

The Hungry in Virjucky

A flap was raised once when someone iggynant and plucky
said consumption is rotten in the State of Virjucky.
The State of what? Kentuckinia?
Were Kentucky and Virginia
suddenly consumptive? or drunken? or overnight
had they gone hungry?
Had they merged? No one seemed to know.
And no one asked Kentucky or Virginia.
Two calls were made. No one answered.
Via slow mogul the Department of Angry Culture,
so unculturedly sure of its cult, issued its talky:
All is ducky, don't fuss, the impoverished Virjuckians
are about to get foodstuffs truckload lucky.
As though the hungriest could be the lucky ones.
The Secretary of Anticulture,
dreaming that his audience was rank on rank of drones,
and that truly all was well in Vijuckiuckiania,
droned on and meaningless on.

Moon McRae

Moon-middled McRae
                    walks big,
                    and stooped,
and (he says) supposedly wise,
having but twice been duped,
up and down and somewhere around
first street in our downtown
and swears he cannot die, ever,
of anything but the big C itself
coursing through him like a river,
he's already been diagnosed,
now he's predisposed
to think on that time when,
unbeknownst to other men,
he shall no longer walk,
being truly and finally stooped,
tall-bent along any street
shuffling long feet,
peering with those neutral eyes
or peering otherwise
or appearing anywise.

Blue Mountain

Blue Mountain is blue.
Blue, from a few miles distant.
Up on Blue Mountain,
Blue Mountain is green, all conifer
green, pine and fir.
An oak or two up there.
Distance dictates green
is blue,
says a sheen,
a certain glow,
says air,
and I say
and you.

Lake Eye Adventure

Lake Eye Adventure in reality is unnamed.
But to see it you drift away
from the aisles of crowds.
Down road. Upmountain a ways.
Span granite.
Into blue, into the silence of clouds.
The apex has risen high. Spy the vista next.
Reach it in five legsteps.
Gaze east and down.
Two high lakes. They are sister cisterns.
Little sister. Bigger sister.
Long might your day be,
but the best of days.
The sisters are eyes, blue with skies,
blinkless, blinkless their upward gaze.
Winking by the twinkles of the night.
Long may your days be,
and the best of days.

Numphrey Thomphrey

did this: He *wished* to live
some kind of life
fully in accord
with the needing nerves within him.
He *wished* not to be bored.
He wished to climb a mountain.
He wished to run white water
no matter the river.
He wished to make love with ten thousand women
and remember each name like a memory of an omen.

                                          Amen.

And track a big cat
and without death at that,
click its picture
and come back home and give a lecture.
Mere conjecture.
And dive for the glittering medallion of danger
in the stirring gray stranger sea.
But Numphrey Thomphrey never moved.
His mother's method had informed his childhood
that life was a diseased id
until it desisted;
comfort was salubrity;
and comfort contorted him
as at his mother's breast.
Numphrey was a knot at liberty.
To quote him: I would love to do those things
but aren't they worth the trouble?

Reverie

Dream'sday.
You see in an airpond of beyond
a happening, a magic.
An serene insistence
idiosyncratic, mystic.
Mind'seye.
You feel in a mental winddrift,
it stirs you
but you are still.
And yet you feel.
A reverie.
Beyond, just there.
There is a where
to it, but where?
And a time to it, but when?
Some kind of untimed ever key
in the soundless clock.

Minon Little and the Fallen Woman

Minion Little is pulling hair
The hair of a woman
Fallen from grace.
In return she is kicking
Minion Little in the omen,
And biting his hand,
And scratching his face.
With pride the fallen woman
Is bound to her place.
But she was bound there
Before she had fallen.
There is a pressing wind above the land
Decrees she may again not rise,
Whore of many, whore of men.
Minion Little is a stone in her prison.
Now he dreams of her furious eyes.

Reston "Mélange" Meland

a believer in extensive variety
who sallied forth in search of it
largely to succeed,
there are so many places,
but unfortunately to fail
in one acute particular:
he found the mind of man
in all those plenty provinces
adhered to material
and to what will cut the flesh

to the dolorous exclusion
of its tidbit
aspiring
mapless
would-be-expanding
cranium-sky
of stars. He said.

Afro Dottie Makes a Triangle

Down our museum hall,
in a chamber of flowered marble,
next to Aphrodite
and the nuptial Nippon doll,
they've set an Afro Dottie
in teak millennial,
armless, afro and all.

Man, have a look.
An empire of lordships
will discard commerce here,
cough casual commentary,
be launched from this her-bor.

Look, the queens stand a facing three
and smiling, and could be forever.
The fragile fingers they don't have,
witness them just touching at the tips
between the delicate and emburdened hips.

Lasaker

Lasaker, fleeing the law
out of middle Ohio
heading west you are.
Lasaker, I can see it.
Without asking her
you will kiss
on the hot run
a beautiful girl on a street in Denver,
beautiful in Denver
as the mountains to shine after you.
You will remember her.
You will ask a coin of an eightyyearold
former whore near the lake of salt
(she made them return
in her youth of blossoms,
they returned bearing leaves,
each leaf a profit and a love).
And you will shake hands in Elko
with a man who can make an engine
sing *La Traviata*.
But Lasaker
in California
the oblivion you seek
shall dream bleak dreams
and you shall sleep
but awaken weary.

Frandon Forsaken

They have abandoned Frandon.
They are away and unthinking,
bound for the where they do not know
and will not find.
Frandon is left to sift the grains
of the natural.
He walks a back road now,
slowly, his head is down.
To his right, arboreal,
to his left, all pastoral.
His walk is the walk of the lost.
His mind is the mind of the wind.

Big Mama Meatball

went about being a mother
by loving all that was
and by endeavoring to include
all that she loved
within herself.
That was the same
as including herself
in all that she loved.
Many of her loves were food
and she and her loves were one,
so love accounted
for her bounty
of ounceage.
But there are no boundaries
on any love founded.
Her children were the universe.
When the mother of the universe passed away
she wouldn't move from her loveplace
for twenty or a hundred men.
And if by chance she had,
no more of her love than an arm
would have cleared the door.
So they went all in and all out,
condemned the building, tore the wall out,
brought her down with a crane
and buried her in a railroad car.
Every ounce was love.
Love is how you tell them who you are.

Meekan

Meekan exits the Gate to Glory
at the state penitentiary
with a grim-set jaw
and remembering eyes.
Eighteen years ago
he swore he would not smile
until he makes San Francisco again
to find the Mazie he loved,
take her at any cost,
love her again at any cost.
But she will not be there.
Meekan smiles early
when for the window of the bus
a roadsign mentions
the love that was.
Praise be
unto all detentions.
He smiles a second time
thinking of the one word "penitent"
in "penitentiary."
Meekan is very penitent, so very penitent at what he lost
each time the parole board denied him and tossed
him away in spite of the intolerable intensity
of the desire he had to regain and hold it.
So very penitent for eighteen years,
now he will kill with enormous joy
enormous joy
to hold it again.

Clinical Social Worker Lynus Klein

Lynus discovered in a clinic
the amount of work there is therein
(enough to make a grown man a cynic),
the piled amount of work there is.
In the office next to his
piles on piles, and the office next to that one,
and the office next to that one.
They were all his offices.
All the work there really is
for a sincere social worker
in an antisocial
oversocialopulated world
is work a ferflumber too cumbersome
for any mortal set of motives.
Lynus, clinic-weary, blearyeyed,
a new intrinsic cynic,
gazed out a window
at all the towers in the world
reared to stand before the sun,
and gazed at all the accomplishing to be done—
enough accomplishing for everyone
in all places
to need a degree in social work.
Would that take part of the load off him?
And should those towers darken the sun,
or should he toil to pull them down
and raise up instead the red towers of the dawn?
He yawned and thought of blissful sleep
and blessedly didn't know.

Nihilist Nemming

Nemming was born out of nothing
into very little of anything
and it wasn't even worth resenting.
But though he lacked for motive
he took to condemning.
And he lacked in expenditure.
Blinking required a feathertip of energy.
Any unworthy thing required Something.
And born out of Nothing
              Nothing
into very little of Anything At All
worth the labor of carriage and expulsion,
whose fool would he not refuse to be,
expending nothing
            nothing
of that so very little?

Sabra and Shatila

Does not the warrior know?
Life is a refugee.
Life is an immemorial mother,
traveler from a leveled hovel
dropping, like tears,
children all in wilderness.
She is queen of being,
yet her subjects
they are as objects
and do not know her,
cannot name her,
are full though
of blaming her,
marauding her mosques,
threshing her flesh,
slaying her babes.
Not yet does the warrior know.
Allah, Father, Lord Nebula,
behold the killcamps,
cadaver, corpse, carrion, flies, flies,
dead one, sleeper, eyes on eyes
shut open,
and silence, dead silent ...
and see, the facelet of this infinite infant
newborn, ancient just this instant.

— *late 1982*

Bismerone Squat

Squat squatted in a thirty-two-year
course in tolerance
in order to learn to absorb
or look around
or duck beneath the sound
of the words he heard and was to hear
about the odd-lipped oddity
embedded in his monicker.
Bizmy believed
in the dignity
even of those
who guffery-guffawed
at his Dismal Alone Scat
as though they knew enough of souls
to laugh at his.
He knew enough of souls
not to laugh at theirs.

Ellie Mae Windoe

nothing but waitress
counter to table
to table to table
and always the night shift
waitress forever
with all she is able.
An expert now at the half-a-flip smile
and the quick-turned back.
Where Ellie Mae works they all come,
coffee costs a coinage,
the coinage buys electric lighting
and a seat, central heating, a certain brightening
of things, a hello today at Ellie Mae,
cream and sugar for the coffee, and a chance at talk.
Ellie Mae Windoe
waitress forever.
But today
is a new forever.
Today a man will enter here
who will peer gently
into the half-a-lip smile
and the turnaway mind,
who will peer kindly
with a blink of sorrow
at her twenty-one years
of waitress forever.
Now let her smile again.
Let her know his face
and return his eyes
and never turn away.

The Dog Man

Every afternoon
for an hour
on the grass
in the park
sits a man in a quiet

to whom come
the dogs.
He sits in a quiet
and the dogs come.
He strokes their heads,
they are gratified,
they pace
slowly away.

He does not talk.
He does not call the dogs.
But they come.
He touches the needing muzzles
in the park
in the afternoon.

He gives an air
of kindness beyond himself.
When the dogs have gone
a squirrel will draw near,
not for the nut.
Only people
leave him be.
That may be kind.

Tomorrow's darkness
over the park today.
A terrier
touched by his hand

is scenting the air.
This little dog
is scenting as well
the onpulsing tempo of things.
Soon it will rain
and the man will not be there.
You and I
will not know.
The terrier will know.

Similarities

A similarity
is a nondisparity.
Not so rare, the similarity.
A similarity and a Sarah T. Lee.
Here is my declarative:
Any similarity
to any person blest or ceased,
noble or humble,
acreak or nimble—
if you love the bee
you love the bumble.

Life Wore Out for Fermann

Life wore out for Fermann
in a stale state hospital
crumbling with the salt of the sea
and moaning with the seawind
of the past.
In a stale state hospital
where certain ravening rodents
lined the shadows in the hallways
and jeered all anguish,
outgrew their gnawing-fears
and nested in his mattress,
and ate his toes at night.
Fermann cried, "My feet are next!"
Technicians fed him pills for fear.
The rodents, watching, chortled in their whiskers,
called them Trepidation Tablets,
and swore they would be of no avail.

Calm Twilight Qualm

The softglow is fading.
Was the day troubled, and we knew it not?
Is the day fallen?
In the rust of dusk
is there peace,
peace in some sweet stealth
in the shadow growing?
Can the murk come unlurking?
Is it daygone time, gloaming
now? And something oncoming dim,
is it felt in her, known in him?
Can some unspied
eventide
come trusted?

Magno Down

Yes, there came a weather,
a breather, and eerie here,
yet no, it can fall no further,
the nestled ear of
magnolia petal,
no further.

Ribbons of Crimmons

Ebton Crimmons was most popular (by popular vote)
personage at the club. Crimmons
had his friends, "them ones."
Crimmons was elected chairman
of the sponsorship committee,
then club secretary,
then treasurer,
president,
vice-president,
and official and unofficial
consultant and confidant.
Ebton Crimmons,
supposedly beloved of all.
The membership missed him when he died.
When he was suddenly
revivified out of death, however,
and risen, and blown by a stiff March wind
through the front door of the club,
those former friends and associates
stared frozen at time and reality and credential,
and uttered not a word,
but sat in their lifetime of silence;
and greeted him not
as they used to do,
but hated him rather
for the tombstone precipitous and oppressive
on their minds beliefless and divested.

"Harmsway" Hammond

His barnacle, he calls his little houseboat, "Truth."
Hammond was one who discovered
physical detriment and potential
physical downfall there hovering
in employment when he went labor.
He was irreverential.
He found the same in unemployment
when he went hungry,
then in re-employment
when he went executive.
Labor directly attacked the body.
Hunger denied it.
The executive state,
implying certain impositions—
brusque punctiliousness,
fleecing anxieties,
the tyranny of timepieces,
the requisite simulation
of an attitude of uber concernedness
over the impending crash of the lock stock
and the barrel,
or over a production failure in Slimpararrel—
the executive state
Harmsway swears from inside his barnacle,
even at its most ideal
erodes the physical body
with falsehood spoken,
deceptions foreboden,
and consumption consummated.
Now take his alternative barnacle Truth for example ...

Cyber

In the cyberworld
an impurity
is unfurled
by the minute.
The whackers
attack with cyberswords.
Safe, they feel.
In cybersecurity
the seeking securitarians
are on a quest
through the cyberworld
for the chumps
within it.
They know
the chumps are there.
They can sense them like dayglow.
But where?
The securitarians
bump cyberclumps,
owwy.
But nothing hurts.

Gusto Gusmusser

Gusto's wife was so beloved
that he wished to ensure
her security even Beyond
and purchased two cemetery plots
at great expense—

after which he was bothered tired
and tossed awake every night for a year
trying to trace and shake away
a great oppression he had acquired.

On the three-hundred-sixty-sixth
morning bright with sun and muscle
he arose with a Bunyan chuckle,
telephoned the county newspaper,
and told the clerk in Classified,
"For a year now I've been waiting to die.
But they don't call me Gusto for nothing.
And as of this moment, don't you worry,
I am back in a hurry
to see this thing out."
And he placed the following ad
in the trade-me column, Gusto did:
"Two cemetery plots
for a tractor."

The Gilliam Funeral Chapel

The Gilliam Funeral Chapel
sleeps twenty-nine.
The many migrant children of being
bring feetfirst the many more
migrant children of having been.
But the chapel has never been full.
Life is clung to, it glows like dawn,
it whispers, it sings, it dances like rain,
and the alive child, young and old, it clings.

Today a bearded passerby-prophet
clad in a single raiment
and walking in sandals
gazed on the chapel.
"The walls of this place," he said,
"will learn molecular multiplication
and walk outward expanding
like the cub of a great beast
in quest of adulthood
and the throne of domination.
Beware abominations,
or here, all the world may lie within."

Umpire Empey

Umpire Empey
held his impartial balance
against all the tossed articles
of anger and defeat and victory,
against all the swung bats of hostility
and fists of frustration.
Against all imbalances.
Against all the rages of all ages.
Whatever happened to Umpire Empey?

Backstop Baggins

He couldn't hit well
or catch well
but he was always there
and ball meant more to him than air.
Although they hardly knew his name
their game was his game,
and he was faithful as time.
Have no doubt,
he stands by yet
with fingerless hands.
Only the victors and the vanquished
can bow out.

Bidmeyer Madison

Madison a man who grew rich
fat
and finally lazy

off the perjuries of the poor
in bankruptcy petitions.

Madison
thought they were lies outright
but they had none.

Then Madison reached the age of forty-four
and autumn came
and leafage fell
in his collect-it mind
as never before

and tired of his years of grabbing
in the bankrupture of the pure,
now was his hour
of wrong and sorry.

Small yellow birdlets fell from the ginkgo tree
none of them a vulture.
They may have been dovelings. May have been
mockingbirds mocking Madison.
But they were the size and held the hover of hummingbirds.

All the humming victims.

Blowtorch Blevins

welder
          and a good one
(any kind of welding, any kind of tool,
fuse a thing with another, two make one,
use acetylene, gas, electric,
the arc intense,
a soldering iron,
even tape and glue
or chewing gum and spew,
he used it, the world would meld).

But let me tell you
the hardest job of melding
he ever had to do
was the merging of his own divergences
at one juncture
into inner enrichment
and the integration of the self.

And let me tell you
he grew into himself
and let me tell you
he was one with him.

Oceanid

She is unseen, but lives encircling. She is water.
There are those who deny it:
The oceans are rising.
The island people are walking their beaches
as they always have. But their sands are narrowing.
They are also fleeing.
Can they feel at home where home is not,
where they are unknown, not understood
as the people of the sandbeach,
as the people of the salt reach,
as the people of the hands in the sea?

The Oceans Are Speaking

The vast heaves and wanes of sea
and sea grays and sea lanes
are speaking a moan of waves and foams,
spills and combs.
A rightness is gone.
Whereon is wrongness?
And why?
And does survival lie
in the old oceanus
globed and enormous?

Maestro Eben Tosus

for forty-seven years conductor
of the famed Yovoslavarian Radio Symphony Orchestra
and one who knew intimately
and loved intemperately
the many musics he performed.
When the time came to die
Eben thought for a way.
He decided on consistency—
dying as he had lived.
If that life had swung wrong
it was a blister too late now
to swing it back right
if he did know how.
So he climbed the podium once again
to depart leading Schubert.
He left himself
on a violin strain.
The audience thought
it was Eben falling
when his hulk of shell
toppled away.

A Certain Fear Is Rising

Ish Muck Shroom is firing missiles.
Across the Sea of Peace
a certain people, the people of peace,
are gazing at the sky.
Long ago now, they learned this fear.
They have lived well with peace.
They have therefore earned peace.
May they live well.
May a missile find nothing, perhaps incontinence.
May ballistics fail.
May the clouds bristle.
May a missile be hated by the winds.

Epistle ends.

wHorse Epileptic Edgar

Epileptic equine Edgar Gelding
must surely have wondered during his whorseness
what advantage there was in enduring
or what there would ever be in life to endure for.
They called him a whorse. He was a horse with fits
and a chronic case of indigestion
whose indigestion was ridden swaybacked.
He stood cold in his Januaries
in a crackboard barn. We know he dreamed of berries.
He never ate an apple.
He had a toothache all his life.
(The only man who ever invented
dental floss for whorses,
Edgar never met.)
Cold in those Januaries in crackboard leisures
he fell into seizures
and shook into warmth.
Fevered in his Julys
and wanting for medical advice
he fell and shook outcryless
into his very own Januaries.
The man he carried endless miles
through the strenuous mountains and squeezing defiles
weighed two hundred and fifty counterweights.
He was counter to all progress.
But Edgar ran on, far beyond the place
where his faith in life gave out.
Humanity marveled to behold the fallen hulk of Edgar
convulsing in a desperate grovel on earth,
like all the lust denied him,
and humankind gaped.
Then Edgar would lie quiet awhile
breathing in huge winds,
blowing flowers from their stems;
then kick up to standing with an Edgar smile

and dip his withers to apologize
and horse's-ass his embarrassment.
No one ever came to stroke his shoulder
and tell him with a lump of sugar
that epilepsy wasn't demoncraft.
A few even stood away and laughed.
But Edgar ran on
years beyond his faith.
And after all those Januaries
it was July that did him in.
He was carrying that freight of man
in the sway of his indigestion
through the strenuous mountains
one more time, crossing a shallow meltflow
when a rock rolled underhoof,
he fell and threw the clencher fit
that wouldn't quit till Edgar quit.
That freight of man stood watching,
and shaking his head, and said,
"Damn you, Edgar, it's a fine time you've picked
to throw a fit on me." But Edgar, defective,
year-burdened, earless Edgar had run on
and wouldn't come out of it
to be sorry again.

A Hot Wind

A hot wind is eater of snow.
Down the creeks the water, snow
a moment ago,
blurbles in gravel and boulder.
Joyous just so.
The smokestacks of manufacture
belch hot winds, fire thoughts,
into the atmosphere, no afterthoughts.
Achoke and croaking, say the faster thoughts.
We are dreaming our gravity
will keep us breathing.
In our seeming, in our dream,
no levity.

Breather Fine

What came to me in the night, abrupt
as a moment, fine as air
in air,
and what went?
And upped?
Or downed?
Or, in its way,
a simple away.
I cannot know it.
For breath it is an elf bereft
and life it touches
on nothing so much as
an instant in air,
a glory of oneness,
riverpond goneness,
the one sleep beyond,
a nothingness such as
nothing, as such.

The Coming

A cloud enveloped the planet
till everyone looked up,
then it billowed open
to announce the Second Coming,
whereafter it dispersed and the warring nations
fell silent in bated anticipation.

Governments, in secret rooms,
plotted how to undermine and overturn
the Power of Primordial Innocence.
Families locked themselves indoors.
Eyes peered at the streets.

A bearded man *did* come, and he rode upon a donkey.
But no palm fronds were thrown before him.
Though the hooves of the burro, bonkety
it came, clattered like bombs on the cobblestone,
no one heard.
The man rode down out of the Gone-Lost Mountains,
the mountains of the earth,
where he had mined a mountainside
for half a lifetime, half a life,
and thought alone on the stars.
A nameless miner was the only Coming,
haggard and laggard, bedraggled and bearded,
lean as a tendon and hungry as a wolf,
discussing madness with the burro and himself.
Though the world waited on,
he was the only Coming.
If he came among us coughing,
if he beat the years of dust
from his hat against his leg,
if he laughed at visions
and muttered about the mountainwind,
if he had forgotten his name,
and if when he looked at us
he saw us not, but through us to the stars,
could we fear him not,
could we think on him?

Spid

There is a shrunken husk of spider
In our little haunted house.
Disrupted eight-of-leg insider,
It has been dead as a catnabbed mouse
For a year. It hangs on a rung
Of its strandy ladder
High in a corner, overlooked as outdoor dung.
It was a silken living thing,
We knew not if the silken sang.
Laid aweigh in its lofty vistarium,
Arachnid style, aloof at its very room—
Top of the sky, a starless scan-the-area'm,
Spid oversees us but Spid is not one of us—
Our indoor kaputnik, quitted and done of us.

— winter, 1976

Airspace

Over a nation
is a nation's airspace.
It is a fair and unseeable lace
ashine with atmosphere,
rainbow and rain
and sun and place,
shoreline and states,
respiration
and straits,
susurrus
aboveroof,
breath in a sphere,
river and here,
mountain and lake,
rainbow and rain
and sun and place.

New Night

There is a new kind of night.
Down upon our gravy lane,
an hour late,
it falls without shade.
And oh are we unglad.
Up and down our ivy drive
it struts like a senses-taker
exclaiming our names.
We think we hear it.
                    As best
we can, we spy through our blinds.
Eyeing nothing, we label it spirits
but know it is alive,
                    and dread
the knock not of the dead
but of the dark, the bolderguest.
Of what sick sin are we so ashamed?
Good night, Grover. Good night, lover.
Tucked in our pillowed protectorates
we drowse with our marrows wide awake,
hierarchless, marked for fire, yes,
dumbwaiters dispossessed
should a shingle shake.

"Dutch" Famish

Dutch Famish, seeing his empire
crumble beneath him, bullet and fire,
called up his henchmen
and issued orders;
but his henchmen had their orders
couched in their pockets,
orders from deadly Deadmark Locketts.
And while they solved for Dutchy
his every riddle
riddling his middle,
strangely Dutch remembered
the little man Burgerlegs
who had no legs
and skated the city on half an oak door,
who once had looked up at him
and pronounced his Dutch anthem:
"Dutch, heed ye this.
Be ye ever so careful on the way up
and up on the top.
I be down here
safely underfoot
and need not fear what you must fear,
the product of building
what you are building.
Dutch Famish,
heed ye this:
Better it be
not to climb up at all."

There Is a Gloom

There is a gloom
attacking a beacon
in Jim Theport's room.
Jim is the beacon.
And he is a port
after the tossing troubles,
bump and bubbles,
of land and sea.
Jim The Port.
Jim believes in a future of light,
in a tomorrow of worth,
in a dignity on earth,
a life we can understand
and cling to,
give ourselves to,
bring the newly living to,
an all-music of caring
we can sing to.
There is a seeping gloom
in Jim The Port's room.

Left Right Left

In Bagbad there is a left,
       there is a right,
       there is a wrong,
there is a middle of center.
And in Bayroot there are a left,
a right, a wrong and a center.
The center is somewhat
left of the right,
and somewhat right of the left,
come all that dies—
come all that survives,
bone and bereft.
In Bellblast and in Bayroot and at the root
there are a left hand and a right,
they meet aclap in every street,
the cause, the contest, the applause *en corps*.

— *1970s*

Public Notice at the Mercy Mint

Beauty is now
The coin of the realm,
Vend us in candor,
Send us in elm.

Yet Beauty groans lonely
As the creature one.

Lovely is now
The groin of the realm,
Trace him unhindered,
Grace her overwhelmed.

Lovely lies lonely
As the lecher one.

Rancor is still
The hand at the helm,
Ply you in conflict,
Cry you in calm.

Rancor dies bonely
For the Reaper one.

Succor is now
The sugar in the palm,
Consign you in tender,
Kiss me in alm;
Lay us engendering underwhile the moon,
We lie onely and upended soon ...
Done-with, sung, amended tune.

Augmented Reality

Well, augmented reality is coming.
Since it is on its way,
I am in hopes it will replace
demented reality, which is drumming.
There is fogmented reality,
and within it, it is hard to see.
There is dogmented reality; it is howling
at moon, at dogdream, at ultrafrequency,
at earthsound, at scent,
at the loved absent.
There is frogmented reality. A frog knows
whether danger grows.
Whither death throes.
There is a treemental reality.
A tree, in its many-year certainty,
whispers in wind a sensed eternity.
There is kneejerkquency;
spare us from its particukneedy frequency.
Perhaps there is a peacequency,
and perhaps, just perhaps, it rings like horror no more,
no more forever.

Williburn Filliby

For as long as he will allow me
I will write about a man
devoid of love.
I am willing it that Filliby
will find what will be
redemptive to him: a shoe,
a hand, a true,
a trilby.
Headlong does he rush at Being
and he will push the rest of us aside seeing
any objective beyond us or above.
No common value will survive
his oncoming merciless survey.
What well he weighs,
and what he loves,
is what he shall devour.
Weakness take the hindmost
and devil take the run.

Bonnet Sonnet

She's quit carnality: It's criminal,
What men do, crouching cat before the lark,
Lord Vulcan vaulting toward eruption's spark;
But trailing union the inimical.
To do, she's fleeing: ought I query where?
It's liberation time. She's free. She dances
Bittercup up a spiny lecher stair
To avert a bra; they're soft as avalanches.
Fear not, Smith, they'll not fall on you, for she's
Abstract, exec, a pink-tied suzerain.
Time long may Suzie reign. Smith, where we've lain
With her, throb off the chillness of her sheets,
We're free. She's flown the nest. Equal, I fledge,
Though I fly not, and fold at Freedom's edge.

Of Her

All these memories of her ...
not quite yet
what was.

Leafboat

Pacific, we have a sometime rain here
wetter than water,
nonspecific, unpacific.
In twenty-four hours
we are engulfed.
We know enough
to swim to live;
the cerebrum knows the ponds.
What I think in delicate rescues for
is that lone runt creature
reaching for life,
one wing or leg garbage, lo
frail arpeggio
upping, plunging
on the redwood scales
midriver, downriver,
lightning skysecting,
thunders exulting,
pluvisaurs resurrecting,
the twinkling of future
a cloudy fount of drown
or a creaking crush
of the flood's choked crutches ...
then the ink wink lingering sure.

Roswell Rummedge

is rifling the restaurant dumpster
with zest, grunt, thump and stir.
His head jumps up and spies me
and his stir and zest
are hush at rest
while his eyes decry me
and watch me by
asking their question,
glaring their explanation:
'Is this another scene, man,
you going to hassle me?
Everybody forages.
You try going a week without a gustable,
like me you'll take to exploregasbord.'

I am past him. The
carnal rule is what?
Eat or you're transmuted meat.
No, scavenger, garbage-ravager,
strange and savage disarranger,
a brassy blast from me
would tend to amount, be tantamount
to carelessy, to blasphemy.
For just down the road from here,
mere hours off, there are razor incisors
lined in a hollow body, fangs in an arsenal,
waiting to slice the human mind precise and contrite
like a fiery ice.

The Erstwhale

Thar whale, embathed and rhythmic fathomer
of sourcewaters, of the free sea womb,
the salt and the surge
of the umbral whelm,
delver of a realm unearthen,
barnacled breaker into sprinkling glister
at the maincrest, in wavy bluster,
a going geyser, flowing sigher,
lagoon crooner, twisting whistler,
schooner-long songster
in pain, pain from yet another harpoon
is hard adive, sounding,
there is no recording
what he is sounding like.
Thar whale's grand father was as long as Baja California
or the Alaska peninsula with a tail of Aleutians.
Evolution's bobbed his flukes a bit
and shrunk him, that he might eat less
and still survive. Survive.
Nevertheless, ever the fewer, his grand, grand son,
thar whale harpooned,
is sounding doomed,
and must rear breaching some hour soon
killer-gray,
sperm-blue,
trying to scream,
beholding with horror's horrendous eye
a flippant fleet of ferrous fishes
ridden with parasites like princes.

Intrinsics

There are distances within.
They are disturbed. Distraught. They are whorls.
There are volumes within.
There are depths.
Attempt to measure them
they turn mist. To measure mist
you must insist
that unreality persist.
The inner nonrealness is not unreal.
It is more like edgeless strata,
laden with meaning.
To measure the meaning
discard the strata. Think strata's sphere.
To measure volume,
measure nothing, solve plume.

The Kibosh

You put the kibosh
on a thing that was a wash
by its very nature in the earliest incipient pie-shlosh
of it.
You know in your thinkjiggery
they cannot love it.
It will not wing, not a smithereen
of lift.
The poor thing is a sad and broken beast
limping monster down Death Alley.
Only a kibosh, a stymie, a quash,
and a thunk on the topnotch
will do to stuff it.
With care, with empathy,
we part with it.

The Nongentleman's Diatribe

I cannot recollect the nongentleman's diatribe exactly
but my the audience thought he lit it with a flare.
I thought he made a spurch.
Perhaps he was saying nothing.
They listened for the nothing and loved him for not saying it so fair.
The only voice was his oratory hum,
till he spoke a word and caustic blurtery spewed like stew
throughout.
I was certain he had said nothing, not one ijjithus of anything at all.
They stared at him from thoughts of the awful.
They stared at him through saucer monocles
two on an aunt's nose, two on an uncle's.
He climbed the stares
into candidacy.
They, the ayes who would see him in,
they, the child consistencies
who were his future constituency,
loved him instantly, you see,
for what he did not insist he would say:
Pain of what that could have been.

Street Question

If we riot
who will love us?
What of quiet?
If soundless we march
will that be a riot?

But we must consider the stars:
the stars of peace
and of brotherhood
and of sistery
and of the true liberty.
We must consider the truth of moons,
the births of suns.

Girl Ursula's Paper to the Ultrapatriot

Earth's peace is larger than your nation, Mr. Bannerman.
You could care a moment, if you only would,
for a fairscore, foursquare, forevermore future
full of flora, flutes, forums, and the forms
of firstling infants unfurling, Mr. Pillager of Pacifists,
        Mr. Deathmaster Fist.
In the lingo of the firmament, Joustmonger Jingo, you are a darkled
        star, marble in your armament.
For your coach it smokes, Mr. War Hoax,
and your way is lonely,
a drain lane, 'bye path, pike of poached bones.
You could care a moment, Mr. Ill Omen,
for a future full of seeing, full of we'll-being,
full of make-lovely-ing,
full of making life ring,
full of ciphering how the zephyr spirals,
full of study how the snowflake sullies,
O Mr. Fog Flagwave, mal-mannered man,
if you would, if you would, if you would only.

Snill's Door

If there were a door
into the right there,
there in front of him,
across the little hill,
the rockish road,
to the bigger little hill,
across the ibbling creek,
to the bigger big hill,
and the blue hill behind it,
into the wind and the wind's will,
into tree, water, sky,
if there were only a door ...
but the door is hugonimous,
and Snill can't find it.

Better Little Bailess

A hundred times we've heard the Bailesses
axing their latest sofa,
rollingpinning a thump-to-do.
Tonight it's little Bailess,
he gets little better,
he'd better be good, he's bloody,
he slips to his room,
locks the door. Goddamn,
it hurts this time.
They rollingpin the furnace,
strike poses, chalk each other's caricature
on the fracas-room wall,
pitch twelve-inch darts at their chalks
of art, of mind and heart
inimitable. Easy targets.
Little Bailess, where he's been before,
listens at the door in a sore dark. Drats.
He bloody better be good.
Voting to stow in a sociable hold
he dons his coat, it might get cold,
finds his baseball mitt, his fifty-cent piece,
and budging bloody mum and slow
opens the prison window.
Someone will go his Bailessness.
Not four hundred yards away is this
crashing freeway rapid
which knows there is a sea.

Trumble the Trouble Bum

Trumble followed
where the problems led,
he had a problem
for a head.
Trouble was fascinating
for all its beauty of anguish and beguiling.
Trouble made the mighty into the humble
and the humble into the numb and the noble.
Trumble followed all of it
and never even stumbled.
And through it all
he was alive and smiling.
And the sun was smiling.
And the cluster-dusted nights were smiling.

Goose

At least, they called him Goose
for his lack of any affiliation whatsoroose
with any creature that brought about feathers.
Goose had asthma and raspmia and cursed the birds
in bursts, words, and thirds.
He said they might as well
have given it to him themselves,
the effect they had on his condition.
But I will quote for you coughing
an article of his philosophy:
"I hate the birdies every one.
When I see one on the windowsill
I wheeze it away. Here no windows ill!
And I cough up hatred in my dreams of talons.
I scorn turkey sandwiches
      and fried chicken
      and roast duck.
But I will allow you to make one tie,
if tie you must,
draw one straight line,
if draw you must,
between the birds and me:
Call it the one Umbilicus.
Call it the Overlife
drawing One Breath
in all the divers forms."

Yoony O'Gruth the Universal Father

He discussed his uncommon children before us
one afternoon in midsummer,
the sun was a far desire.
He told us his children
have eyes as bright as moons.
He told us they are short and tall
and anybody you might name.
He told us they are starving and obese
in the starlit west, in the sunrise east.
He told us they hate and love.
And he told us those children
will derive toward heaven
from the quaffing root,
take bud and burst into blossom,
and plunge from the bough again
forever.
Someone, from a fog of puzzlement,
asked him "How many children do you have, O'Gruth?"
"Gruthillions, gruthillions," he answered,
smiling at some far horizon.

Zipsip Smithers

Zipsip fell away one day
abstaining from maintaining
and his uncle found him in a bottle
under the boardwaddle.
Lord Uncle, sang Smithers,
the days were all foul weathers.
The birds were all fowl feathers.
Lord Uncle, sang Smithers,
do you remember Annie Orward?
I have mislaced her come-hithers,
she is on to others, gone thethers.

So he would be henceforward
no one but Zipsip Smithers
who could bleed a bottle in a sip
and sleep the battle
under the boardwaddle
and whose ear couldn't hear his lip.

The Arrival of the Wind

The wind has arrived here, soft and steady.
I listen, it is singing;
there is a meaning,
it is seeming.
I listen, ear-ready
and alert.
There is a sibilance.
It is songlike
but untonguelike.
I cannot make the words,
but there is a meaning,
it is seeming:
I come from there,
I come from them,
they have dreamt,
they are watchful,
they are listening,
they are well,
they are hurt.

Though Leaf and Cloud

Although the oakleaf rides
breeze to earth, and the clouds flow gone ...
though these are done things, done ...
something, a something—time—unhumming, abides.

Quoncy Quondam

Quoncy took ill of the mad he went
when he finally fired his father's mighty 30-.06
after 30-.06 years of holding out for peace,
and heard the ricochet.
The mad he went
was looking for it.
"Cruel fool in me, soldier, bandit, policeman
somewhere within me, I have fired!
What did I smite but what I have admired?"
There was a core of life, he was sure,
yes, there was a core of life
created and unbelievable and pure,
yet he had taken arm and fired.
What could he have broken,
what could he have burst apart,
what could he have shattered into shadows
but what no man might reassemble,
treelimb, lifelimb, lung, heart?
There was nothing out there anywhere
awaiting any bullet shrieking in air
but was some sort of life, a nature-sort of fair.
So Quoncy had stricken life into prehistory.
But had it breathed a tiny cloud of mystery
into the quietening air?
So he lifted boulders.
"I know there's a round around here,
Life is where, Life is where."

Our Lady Infatuated

This time is like a lady infatuated with a mirror.
She peers. She marvels at her face.
But a glimpse and glance
should have informed her ignorance
in two instants:
She shall be beautiful forever,
she is a thought in the Mind of All that Is,
movement in Its stillness,
grace in Its glowing waste,
the Now in Its Infinity chase.
And we, her younglings hungry,
her divided and sundry
granules of ambition,
flares of ignition,
we charady maidies, we your avarice joes,
do reside, like sands ahurl in a blow,
in a wingèd mansion all aglide,
not down a wholesale avenue—
but up a starry blizzarding
out a snow of suns ...
touch such wizardry,
haven't I, haven't you.

The Speaking Tree

We have a speaking tree
on our mountain of many trees.
I listen carefully, four carefullies,
there. But what speech,
these treely outreaches each?
I listen five carefullies.
But I cannot, not quite, get it.
It is there in these outreachlings
of the tree.
But the tree, it is speaking tree.

Across Our Valley

Across our valley stand the hills
and the mountains.
We see them well.
They tell their natures
in the air,
tell of their statures.
Good air there,
shouldered by Grizzly Peak
and its cat-wild partner
on the ridge.
There was an honor
in the bear,
now where.

Peanut Johnny Explains His Repoor Card

from his class in world history.
Mom, I'll tell with precision.
It's my instructor Mister Istorian.
I hate his story not because it is his or even
because it really isn't
but because I am John
and the story is not mine.
I've read his story—every fuming line.
And Mom, his story goes on and on.
Colossus conquered the colosseum.
Redundance rose and holocausted him
and Colossus took his lossus.
There was peace among the little folks
for sixty-six or more whole strokes,
then along came the wrongmaim army pokes
of rude King A Long Arm,
wreaking ready headspins
in their antique skins.
Istorian salutes the flag of glory on
throughout his mangled pages.
Bespangled in the gore of yon
his heroes romp into the ages.
Mom, good madam, I sorely dread 'em,
Mister Istorian and his classic behead'ems.
I cringe as far back in the academ
as I can creep quietly, ravaged by rages.

Holiday Harrimac

"Holiday" who fast and faster kept going on them
finally at long last could not return
his bloody nose to the gritty grindstone
but audio'd his boss a letter on the phone
from a lodge in Wickiup
called The High-Up Rye Cup:

Dear former sir:
I exult to inform your
exaltedness that I have spat the metal
tongue-depressor from my teeth, finer's the fettle,
and that now I choose to lose my muse
in the clarity of a rarer atmosphere
and in the process of disremembering you,
sir that once you were,
and I have of late, and in great measure,
in life found pleasure.
You tried so hard to keep life from me.
Why? Did it terrifrighten you so,
that someone near you might come alive,
come brightly alive like a sunrise
after a stormy night;
and you might not?
I think I have discovered
Life warrants no fear,
it shines like fire
but touch it, no harm,
only warm,
and waking,
and dear as its form.

For Schelly

You will never need to ask
what task it is or it is not
the formless wind plies at.
By part not half
will you need to know
toward what void to come and go
Time turns you so.
There is nothing but loving: know.
There are no wars.
There are no fears.
There is no fleeing.
And there are no years,
there but one moment being.

This Guy, the Ex-Vagabond

Yeah, this guy went everywhere,
I mean everywhere.
And then he went everywhere
he had been before.

What is it about going,
even though you'll never get there?
If you're going everywhere
you can't be anywhere,
you're in too many places.

So this guy had been everywhere
and decided to try some here-y where,
and bought a cottage on the coast.
Now this guy's cottage has a porch—
that's where he's sitting, coast and porch,
cauterized from the heart out,
heeding such crafts as pass and seem to pass
in the offshore night,
heeding boyhood, and sea with no land in sight—
dreaming of distance.

Employment

It is like this ghost, see, shadowing your blythe
nature with a wherewith scythe
in one bone hand, the other full of blank checks and stock shares
in a black-cape pocket; cowl over eyesockets.
Employed, you don't know it's there.
Unemployed, for the whole duration,
look over your shoulder, soldier you're haunted.
When the old wind blows and the rain comes colder
your ghost becomes a moaner.
"What's that you're moaning, ghouly host? Is it Wind, wind?"
The ghoul drools on: "When, when?
I await your yeses. I am a Necessity of the age.
You are but a child of your time—and slave to hunger.
Whhenn? Whhenn?" The night howls the ghoul's growls.
Let us exemplar: Enyark Swargler passed away.
At his winter interment appeared the Ghosts of His Past:
There stood Happiness, a fry of five;
Grief and Woe, *fraterna* and *sorora* close and supportive,
deplorers of forty;
Accomplishment, a lad of twelve;
Leisure, gleeful toddler all of two, most of three;
Freedom, a savagehaired radical
juvenile transgressophile bound and shackled,
still gasping for air;
and then Employment, Employment,
old raven-caped whitebearded frightful giant looming over all
oh, eighteen feet tall,
glooming in some high bereavement
above the sleepstone steep in its easement,
above the ept earth's ebon yawn.

Rabbit-Ears Rayburn

Rayburn was once Rabinowitz.
He says it is safer to be weak and quiet
than to read aloud among the powerful.
Rabbits-Ears, I'd best tell you,
was at the wrong end of Your Rope
in nineteen-forty and in 'forty-one.
They will batter down your adores,
he says, rush in, half-notice you,
laugh "Pass him by, those are rabbit ears,"
roar off venomous, heinous, intravenous,
warriors on a spearoid.
The rabbit, successor to the thorn,
out of earshot as his ears would have it,
creature of ignominy and habit,
shall have steadfasted everlastingly
in his leaves beneath the irecraft sky,
distinguished as a toadstool, but passed by.

Bank Robbery, Dallas, 1970 —
a Statement by the Guilty

We have ascended the pursestrings
suspended from the portals of your palaces
like fine vines, and entered the ballroom
inviolable, lion-guarded, vault-doored,
because we are abhor-ified by your having and our having not,
and we desire to have,
and we hate you for the anguish you exacted of us
when we approached your luxuriance
with shovels, observance, and lawful subservience.
Forgive the utter resolve within our hunger.
Forgive the violence born of that hunger.
We were trying to burn a hole through an iron paper wall.
For yesterday, when we held our hands before our eyes,
all that we could see
was parchment wrapping pencils of bone,
and under the bone,
tomorrow's night, breath of earth, scope of stone.

Mistaken Drake Aicken

Aicken was wrong and mistaken for so long
they said he didn't know right.
Aicken said he not only knew right
but he knew it better than they
from having failed to do it for so long
he could spot a wrong all year long.
Aicken refused to guarantee
his next undertaking would be unmistaken
but he did declare quietly with a placid pulse
he did know the darks and results
of where he'd been.
And where he'd been was his Drake.
Which was all the immeasurable value
of a mistake.

Hillogene Delfa Burnsmable

She says, "I'm as black as I'm able.
I try to be as loving as I'm black.
Loving is a hard skill to learn.
You have to learn it through the hate.
If you fail to learn it or you learn it too late
to let the others know you've learned it
you have to die up and come back.
Today I wrote all presidents a letter
and sent all tablechiefs a cable:
I said the lovinger is the greater
and all the daylongs of time can be better."

New Is the Flower

All the flowers along Mystery Lane
have come up plastic.
They wave their price-tag petals,
with sell-us fanaticism,
a stiff-kneed spastic,
repellent nonsplendor,
in each wee breeze.
You see, the fairy flowers are turning peddlers!
Your bugle beckons where the battle isn't.

Assassination

The lions have splintered their cages in a fury
and murdered another Gandhi.
She wanted roses.
In eastern Europe the secretmost police,
no moon in their gloom,
not a streetlight to hate by,
not a wick's wink, not a firefly,
have garroted a priest.
He was of the people and wanted peace
please, perhaps, soon, at least.

The agent, the assassin, the annihilator—ageless antagonist—
is a knife beyond nightfall,
missile in the dripping mist,
powder cloud in the milling crowd,
sworn in creed, religion, loyalty and blood
to neutralize the adversary.
Leader of humans, beware, be wary,
he is everythere, everywhere,
and he is heart-full
of his hard ardor.

And what of the people?
What the people wish for, pray for, dream of,
is no, no, not another martyr,
but the ever of that shootless blossom
down the pathway, yonder,
taproot in the wellspring
where the unborn are gathering
even now, in their silence awesome—
how it thunders at the portal
of the air, of the light,
to enter of the father
through the maiden, through the mother,
into the garden beyond wonder,
none other, none other.

— probably late 1984

The Hour Moment

An hour ago
a moment began.
The moment required an hour
to be a moment fulfilled
and a moment waned.
It was an ultraoddity.
Some unknown moment prodigy
came gliding.
Something meant something.
What it was, well,
I groped for it,
but it was a forage without result.
No hope for it.
The hour moment
was long in rising, long abiding,
and as I foraged for it,
among my antennae, amid my meanings,
in my files, behind my siding,
by some wise I knew it
unfindably subsiding.

February 20, 1976

A degree or two, two slices, of Pisces.
Three hundred sixty degrees of sunlight—
except in the Rocky Mountains, knock-scarred
and block stark,
where a snowstorm is rolling trucks,
they came up boxcars,
in a game of luck.
The birthday girl,
the frail one an army abducted,
sits in the courtroom watching it happen.
As it happens half the others,
the projectiling objectors, the warriors,
the sisters and brothers
are dead by volley, dead by fire.
The slender girl is still alive.
They are courting her.
She is moved, not wooed.
Maybe, full of food
and covered with mud,
she weighs a hundred pounds.
I say Weigh on.
A hundred pounds of Life
beats thirty of bone.
Alive is how to be.
It beats a slow chauffeuring in a patrician hearse.
She sits in the courtroom
watching it happen.
It happens. They spirit her
from one hideout conundrum
unto another, to the thump of one drum:
the brusque pulse of justice.
Sure, why not, she is a basketball,
they drivel her down the court,
back and forth, south and north,
score too, score for, score against ...

The attorney for the defense,
Your Honor, says it's a madhouse
out there, drive down the trade routes,
drive down the glad rows,
drive down the shade roads,
count the bars across the windows,
count the barrooms and the shots in those.
She curls in the court womb
watching her transformation,
absorbing the barnstorm,
nearing her renascence.
Yes, what we must speak of
is madness, the misappropriations
of warlocks, the joint thiefs of stuff,
the suave slave labialists await in the lobby,
the unforghettoble children,
the forsaken darknesses of closets,
the captor-general's two eyes of flame,
the taperecorded hatred
speechmade for all posterity:
masks of one nightmare
not awakened from.

Mackwhack McGeever

Mackwhack, an old family misgiven name
from long ago in the McGeever tree.
It turns up every few generations or so.
And yet, as Macked and whacked as Mackwhack was,
he had another frequent fluther, this buzz
what-does-ing in his ear, "You say you do *what?*"
Mackwhack was a linear calibrations expert
but no one knew what he *did*.
He inverted the uninverted,
recalibrated the inversions,
averted various sensornips with pure alertness,
and recalibrated the very nodes of circuitbodes.
And tired O tired
did he grow of explaining.

Seedhead

A seedhead has a philosophy.
A thing grows,
seeds,
spreads.
A thing needs.
A touch,
a wind,
a having been
and an about to be,
make a growing living thing.
A thing free.
In a certain seedneedy
concealing of glows,
in a certain reseedy living
science of silence
the seedhead knows.

Eyerises

With saucers of eyes
good friend Arnie Thay
brought two irises
exclaiming, "Aren't they!
Aren't they!"

Ol' Papa Maybe, the Incredible Shrinking Man

Papa Maybe discovered in his eighty-third year
he had sunk from six-foot-four
to a sunken six-foot-two.
He took the next year off from his retirement
to think about that drop in stature.
At the end of the year he was six-foot-one.
How had he shrunken and what had he done?
Ol' Papa Maybe
had a whole community of friends
who struck his door for advice at every opportunity,
and although he was prone
to whole discourses of "maybe"s
that community seemed to benefit from it.
After the twelve months off from his retirement
he was able to hold forth on senility
with wisdom, authority and prehensility.
"Senility is a time to learn returning, maybe,"
he would say, rubbing his new baby whiskers.
"You will probably shrink a little wink.
You will need to think on that, maybe.
You will realize that it's more
than a softening of the muscular,
a ticking of ligaments
and a settling of the junctures.
It is the beginning, maybe,
of the regal return into the night
unfathomed, unimagined, enrapt."

Elevenoaks Elfwell

He used to drive a school bus
back in Hollobooyas
in the A.D. 1930s despite a skewedness
gnawing within. He delivered the screaming children
faithfully. All he could view from the end of his run
was the roadway leading in clear abandon
into the sunset west. He had to turn back east, confound it,
toward the county compound.
But New Alba True was just
thirty miles to the untried west.
It was beautiful in May when he kept on going.
A few miles outside Chili-Come-Chilla
he sanded the county lettering off the sides of the bus.
With the new paint it read Boo Count Elfwell.

Speculatively proceeding for the glimmering Pacific
he wasn't that far from being there
when that old engine chugging up a heated hill
in the land of scrubgrowth and steadfast liveoak
couldn't take any more and blew skyhigh broken.
Elfwell pulled it over and made a home of it
and he's still there selling junk from his roadside rust farm,
stuff he's gathered from a few miles of roadway,
from a few abandoned cars.

In the A.D. 1940s the authori-tories from Elevenoaks
just down the road a ways drove out to move him on
but Elfwell charmed them with philosophy and wit
and they decided he was a local asset, not a detriment,
and he might draw business to Elevenoaks.
They did come out with equipment and mokes
and move his bus home back forty yards.

But it was true. Even today the whizzersby
pull off at the rusted bus to buy

a bottle or a bucket of bent nails
and behold this bearded flower of local color,
and hear his voice on the aches of the day,
the wars and the unemployment and the fairness of pay.

Elfwell might gaze at you and say
that your sad way or your bright eyes
tell him you have a beautiful soul.
Please live accordingly.
He might say that he was trying to do the same—
live accordingly, aboard an old bus.
The only thing he had ever done wrong was to steal the bus.
He had been making up for it with advisories and consults
for the general betterment of man ever since.
He can see by your eyes
you are the life-form over a beautiful soul.
You should come out at night,
the weather's almost always good,
the sky is as clear as the soul should be,
come out at night and recline with him
upon his luxurious tractor wheel,
and watch with him the many many stars.
He knows exactly how many will be winking.
And he knows exactly that he cannot say why.

The Shop of Rivinnitso

Waldemar Rivinnitso has a shop of clocks.
Daily he is in there with the ticks, the clicks, the snicks.
His only stock is clocks. A few wristwatches in docks
under glass. Daily he is there. Though not every Sunday.
Some days, in the morning, he mutters "O these clocks ... "
A customer will ask, "Beg pardon?"
Their only answer is his eyes.
In the afternoon he mutters, "O these clocks that do ... "
A customer asks, "Do what?"
Rivinnitso shrugs.
Later, not a customer to be seen
in The Shop of Rivinnitso,
he blurts "O these clocks that do
click the minutes O."

C.T. Beesby

C.T. knew what it was
to be high up and officious
and he never suffered from vertigo.
C.T. knew
what a contract was
and how to enter one and wait and see
and how to make corporate ends meet.
He spoke the executive
and administrative tongue
underwriting and conspiring.
But he always insisted
he planned on retiring
sometime before he went to sleep.
And he always said there were bees in "Beesby"
asking to be kept and he knew what a buzz could be.
Signing mergers was only business.
Keeping bees was beesiness.
But time and highrise,
the urging currents of burden
and the conference table resisted.
And the only bees in Beesby
were those he would never keep,
sudden comes the falling
and the little fallen sleep.

Rage

Rage is staring scarlet-faced
at the barrier fence it has misemplaced.
The barrier fence rises before it and enrages rage.
Rage cannot remember building a barrier fence.
Rage can remember a craving to dismember.
Rage appears, axen,
the afeared stare waxen,
disbelieving, then disappear as best
they can, terror twisting their insides.
The very insides of the alive.
The barrier means that the ageless rager, scarlet
of face, a bloodletting upright carcass,
cannot speak. Across the barrier,
rage's victims-to-be, might it be,
speechless, noiseless, in a patience that is terror,
are burrowers in shadow.

Spokesperson

According to the president,
all that we surmised would worsen
has arisen in the purest morning light
improved, behooved, struck innocent
by the dunderhead miracles of wonderment.
The bank accounts
are yanked about
by the hollowgarchs
no more. The missing funds
have been returned. The follygarchs
have fled offshore.
There have been no crimes in the darks,
merely peace, and the lilts of shadowlarks.
All is bettered and all is well.
All are unfettered and freedom is unfelled.
The children are at their lessons.
Now I'll take questions.

Old Stir

For what faint whyfore has W. Wretched Ness,
El Deatho, vexed with very existence and wishing extinction
O so much, not found
as yet his own funeral and good ground?
The squash squads are squelching mass acres of squealers
in Palace Time, a massacre macabre staccato.
It is peasant season in El Salvage War:
surrounded by bloodhounds, scared numb of squanderguns,
in qualm of quislings, the quiet quarry quails in the quagmire,
as yet unquelled, but in vain would it quicken
from the quarantine, the quandary, the draw-and-quarter.
On the Afghan long-piled carpet,
from huge tanks of die, pours a new Afghani stain.
In his cold old motive, why has W. Wretched Ness,
the Deleterio Worm, The Abhorigine, Nephew Nefario,
not perished in his punk pointlessness, not found
as yet in this vast cinderarium
his one encalmment mound,
not one enscraption
worth his slumber under?
Behold him now: he is
as he early was,
forever at variance,
a singleton streak of silver at the temple perchance,
yet as the victims vanish the vile vendettan
is well unelderly, virile, feral, prolongedly wrong,
whooping it up, fight on, glee whiz,
die on, the whole horror long.

— 1980s

175

Two Moons

Last night, over Oliver's Peak, in the south, hung a half of moon
in gentle gold.
But over Cockroach Rise, in the north, hung another, a half of moon
in easy orange.
There was something newly askew,
but I couldn't figure it, I tried to,
but I misreckoned,
I miscalculated, foggily I noggined.
My reckonings were of the earth-surface,
botched and nervous.
I required the cosmovectorings
of elsewheres, misaligned, twisted, curving away and versus.

The Eaten Mount

Through a glacial swirl of smoke
easing circular,
airward or earthward,
teasing gray-blue circles
around Eaten Mount,
a stare from the mount,
I see it there
because I stare.

The Philosophy of Bayleaf Bailey

Bayleaf cooked away at a bean and a leaf
and soup and a sandwich of beef
throughout his life. At least
he claimed that was why he was cooking—
for just about everybody looking.
Bayleaf said
it was indeed a rare head
that he wouldn't cook for:
he wouldn't cook for
any mudhearted bloodrunning murderer
and he wouldn't cook for
any murderer's furtherer.
He would prefer not to cook for
any man of hatred. But then hatred,
Bay stated,
did no harm but alarm
prior to the detonations it gave over to
down at the end of the living arm.
So he would cook for any man or woman
who stopped short of slayhem
or short of mutilation.
Creeds didn't matter. Neither did station.
Bayleaf had seen enough of difference
to know how to simmer with deference.
His stance was not stiff.
It bent in the winds like a leafmotif.
And a person's epicurean palate
wasn't the person's pattering tongue—
common domicile to the contrary.

Choochoo Chimpson

Choochoo, brakeman for the northeast pacific
railway freight express
for thirty-eight years
is making his retirement speech.
He says, "It's this way.
Such is our ongoing,
we may not know
why the iron wheels turn and throw,
or what power it is that turns them."
He says, "It's this way.
We are born and breathe,
we love and laugh,
we hate
              and cry,
early we stray
and late we learn,
we live and we sigh and we die,
the long heavy iron just rolls and rolls,
the long heavy iron just rolls."

Grègoire Alain Guillory

Is this the man who wandered over France
and Germany and Poland and no man's land
during and long after the heinous war,
long after the nations had rebegun the dance
and relearned laughter,
is this the man who wandered after,
who wandered over lands
lying harmed, lying rubble,
in search of the last of his eight children,
the only one he wasn't certain
was dead, because you cling fast
to what is left of life
with what is left of yourself?

The Shooting of the Swayers

Mostly, they were young.
Their ears were attuned to song,
they swayed slightly with what they heard.
The shooter was their neighbor,
yet of a world in horror,
and he sought murder. In the night of song
he found it.
The killing ground, it
suddenly grew heroes,
savers of lives,
retrievers of the bleeding zeroes
of damage, the shrapnels of dishappening,
and the malevolent vortex
drew in more heroes, more savers
of lives, more humans—firemen, wearers
of badges, paramedics.
It was a black hole suddenly aglow.
The high assassin saw no glow.
Random it came riding, the vandal's
thought-saddle of evil, virtual hatred, real bullets
in the horrid darkness ...
given over now to the one light of candles.

— October 5, 2017, after Las Vegas

Stormway Stemmons

Stormway was unblest with a storm thing.
Any word from the likes of heaven
and Stormy did a worm thing
and a warm thing.
What else could a born thing
do in a cold and a blowing
but find the familiar under the foreign
and go about knowing
once again the inherent flame flowing
and the hallowed form of the thing?

Rapunzel Runsumeer

Rapunzel Runsumeer
was O a running Runsumeer
who couldn't quit running
from the tear
she felt the falling
of which was near.
Her question, could she only
have asked it, would have been enthralling:
Was a tear
worth a fear,
was her fear of the tear
not worth her staying here?

Masseusse Ulla

Lovable Ulla, sipping a fine tea,
set eye on her thumbs and fingers,
saw fingers and thumbs and fumbers and twingers,
and began massaging at the ripened
very hour of ninety
years of clear enlivenment.
Under those wise old fingers
and the soft, swift drum
of those palms like psalms
her clients moaned.
The soul of lovable Ulla
moaned in return.
The very hour of ninety
years of thriving
was the hour she was born.
At a hundred and ten
she was hardly worn.
Those moans of love
came back to her
and meant to her
the love she gave.
It was a long way
to the grave.

A Statement in the Spring from Spiffris Reavis

"We have grown hard against the time
and cold against the snows.
There was a law of survival:
We had to deny the wind upon the eye.
Yea, it was a winter did us quiet.
The eye, however, must water through its blindness.
The soul, however, the spirit, the speechless ice,
must melt from the formless flesh to die:
a futile endeavor into idleness,
since all that is, and all the dust that was,
and all the air that will be, lives and is.
Turn you true then, and look with love
at what passes, at what is so quickly passing
yet cannot not be,
never can not be."

The Whisper

Upon a time it was, you visited the mountains shining in the light,
granite of the remembered rope and the hand knot,
trees of the still freeze and the soaring free,
the waters of the leaping glitter, of the roars, of the songs.
And there was a wind sound,
beloved of the trees and the climes above the ground.
It is a planet's whisper, of the color green, of blue,
of granite gray ... a windsigh and hum.
Long is that breath, slow is that sigh.
At home now, long after, in your dreams,
the old whisper comes,
the wind in what trees within,
that very whisper once again, it seems.

Or Old, Is It?

An echo of winter
and of the Oldes of All,
are you, emittance,
are you, crow's call?

The Reverend Dr. Deacon Pastor
Prophet Father Guru Flynnwaid Swade

Flynnwaid Swade entered the tragic profession
many times over, and many times again,
resolved to defeat catastrophe
with reaffirmations and sacraments
and optimism and amnesty.
He was faith-wide Flynnwaid.
Catastrophe defeats optimism.
But Flynnwaid would go on, he was faith-wide,
go on plowing the steeples under the peoples,
translating discredited sealost scrolls,
meditating the One Unbeknownst

until the souls were found
the cornerstone sound
the gods mortal
and the men eternal.

Minkelheim How

Where would Minkelheim have gone,
say you,
after his all went, and he was lost in finding,
and could not, seek where he may,
scent how he might,
could find not?
And say you,
how would Minkelheim
have dreamt in night's mime,
out there
in somewhere,
in his ongone saga
of sleeping on logs
in the hills of hope,
on banks of rivers
ingling by,
sprinkling time?

If It Is of Us

If a certain fairness is of us,
my gentle neighbor nearness,
shall we not bestow our hearts upon it?
Shall we not dream for it
a future begloried
with dawns, noons, nights
and the visits of the stars?
And in the deeper night
when the fight creeps,
when the fang leaps,
shall we dream naught for our fairness
but peace, a song-sing
that the mockingbird tweeps
in its bird dark,
tweep-a-churreep, leem-loo-leeeps
of the unseen shadow
unhurried, of the heard lark.

Brood

Seven stories under heaven's mountain
in twenty-something odd lavatories
the lava techs are steaming open
an eruption fountain
mushroom clouding
gusty unhousing
carcasscount carousement.
Eight stories under a bombin' nation's labyrinth
are ninety lithe lab-rechauns, lately alive,
inhately headless to their freight intrinsic;
frosted with firearmistry forensic
they accost what they must do: moss and mold
and the dying of the crawl.
Thus far they've mist enshrouding all.
I am going to park me an evening on a stone
and ask the ozone what it is ensleeving.
I am gone with no cause to misbelieve in.
I am going to rock while the sunset is grieving.
My right pride and my base dishonor
I am of man, planned in the cosmal godhead
or random as a swept spark
struck of dust among the stars
in the dusky hush of eons.
The moonglow coals away into spun gloom.
Far down the mountain, through the unheard firs,
snarls a nite pride of neons;
farther, up the fountain of air
in hasteless space, no eye blinks
in the moon's mishappened mask.
The scars of old birth,
fire showers when the born babes cried,
are the sockets without eyes
in the face of the sphinx.

Sellabration

I notice a company which has uncaged a lark.
Since the door to the showroom floor
has been kept open after dark,
sales, drummed up, have come up twenty-five percent
a thrively smiley wily ascent
to a high-rise mark.
Making sale for Port Saint Fortune
is the choicest course that life affords one.
Someone, it seems, believes it.
Make heavy sail, once penniless urchin,
o'er the lurching Dividendia Sea.
Now they celebrate, thirty salesmen,
no saleswomen, only two salespersons,
how celibate. Each salesman
grips in one hand a groggy talisman.
Now it worsens.
My feller sellers, it is Auld Lang Syne,
a wheezing Old Lung Sign,
wasn't youth fine,
till the yellow gets up.
When the yellow gets up
they claw drawn the drapes
with their eyes hung in cups,
thirty soused nocturnal apes.

Sally Vashus

Sally Vashus was her stageous
nom de sensatious,
she the stripper for the eyes of men
until the wrinkles
played her out.
But during every show
her eyes stripped men
silent, don't you know,
silent of all the lung they shout.
A woman disrobed before them
and they sat one,
it was a boyhood recome.
A woman disrobed before them
and they stood dumb
and troubled,
and stared
and all but cared.

Twelve poems

out of the rains of parting

Heart

Sitting here on the hill with you, and you apart,
I feel my heart
heaving me to,
waning me fro.
Strange thing the heart:
a monarch, one lord,
in the chamber of onward.
A such of Onely.
A clutch Alone.
In accord or in discord
with all you've ever known
it will follow its own,
hallow its only.

— October 5, 1989 and October 13, 2017

Dogwalk

The dogwalker is passing by again.
Walks his dog among the stones.
He's gimpy in the left
leg, arm, and hand.
He's trailing a strand
of spiderweb from his hair ...
he walked right through it but couldn't feel it ...
now a part of his brief excursion,
it sprinkles glints of silver
where he just was
in the fall light
in the noontide air.
Weighing nothing, all but invisible,
his shadow which he does not cast,
it's destiny's iron gossamer, you see.
Whence he will go, it's
going. He doesn't know it's
there ... but it's there.

— October 7, 1989
Tulocay Cemetery, Napa, California

Talisman Talisman

I have tried to conjure an incantation—
incense, rescind-ogram, Inca notion, ink of potion—
for undoing the done.
I have consulted with the coven coveys
aflutter and trilling in the haven trees ...
with the splaying wavelets of the River Eel ...
with the silken moon and the milk between the stars ...
with the leaf-egress of autumn
when earthtime
flips with a snap
its flowing cape.
Nothing. Nothing.
—Beyond the clutch of this ignorant knave
who gazes now upon his human hand:
the enabling thumb, sensate fingers
how they hang numb, how stone they dangle.

—October 8 and 24, 1989,
and October 13, 2017

Admission under Autumn

Under autumn's golden wrap
I am a warped recollector.
The beauty of our blue-pearl orb,
blessed and bewatered—
of which we are part,
part heart, part light—
is deep, high, flung far.
Well do we know it within.
Yet, idiot
before specters,
I am half quit of it.
Which is the wrongest wrong.
Wherefore this grimacing imbecile
acknowledges he must relearn, keep faith,
entune himself again—
come to love as once he did
what is to be loved … cloudwhorl, whitecap,
warbler, eye of woman—
every sacred leaf of autumn
breaking away from the whispering limb,
making off, flitting gone,
taking leave of what brought it.

—November 3, 1989 and October 13, 2017

Fallen Tear

This pearl of dew
out of the heart of me
about the Gone of you
will arrive at earth perhaps
on a grassblade aching upward fast
into the light, a green gasp
at the glow.
The tear, an infinitesimal icarus
in the infinite, will perish,
surely, in the sun.
And he who let it fall
will motivate away,
implode into the light,
metamorphose,
fall a fate away,
dispose into time.
That is the way it is with us.
We are wafters away.
Somelittlewhere, for an instant
only, no one listening,
our name whispers
after us, a sibilance of vesper.
And yon, beyond us,
the ginger gaieties of spring, hum
of summer, the pale aurora of autumn ...
the occult planets tumbling on
from the anteoriginal fingertip of ought
that tossed the awful,
whence were born the marvels.

—*December 24, 1989 and October 13, 2017*

The Oaken Rose

Once, in Tulocay,
I flashed upon a rose
high up, burgeoned scarlet
from the gnarlèd bough
of yet another
showered, droughted
mother oak.
The wanting-to-believe-in-
miraculous-beleavements in me
had me crane upward to ascertain
it was there and there undoubtable
blushing in the oakknot roost
and I could trust
in the highly improbable.
Though I knew enough not to.
What would be so alien,
what statute subsalient must make fronding foes
of fortress oak and fortnight rose?

But only in my mindgulf
null and awesome
had any ruby rose
come blossom.
Not there even
the oak unbereaven.

—February 10, 1990
Tulocay Cemetery, Napa, California

Pinwheel

Morninglight, eventide, by moonveil and day
the whimsical zephyrs of Tulocay
play spin-your-pinwheel.
I watch it spirit inchmeal spinny.
In me it is one twist of many.

—January 21, 1990
Tulocay Cemetery, Napa, California

A Slaking

From the sunken vessel
vacant of flowers
in the cement memorial
to one clement and gone,
one lone
quick robin dips and drinks
from the pool of passed showers
in the Realm of Things.

—February 11, 1990

Starstep Sonnet

I, being irreconcilably of human
Nature, and witness to the bearing off
Of true men and of beautiful new women
Into the infinite bedimmèd gulf,
Am not, Greatness, whole-soully and all approving,
Though I genuflect and whisper it most humbly.
Existence in itself is an anomaly
Adrift the Void: a fool be disapproving.
The way of things is quitless and on course.
Birth ... Death ... Onwardness endless and away.
Orbit. Bloom. Consummation and decay.
Starforger I quarrel not in my remorse.
For I as well stand dumbling and dumbfound
Before Thee and Thy starry swirlingground.

— April 15, 1990

Stayed

Full-half-crescent-new of moon.
All out of tune
with the new noon of flowers
and the twittering birdsong darts
is the skewed and unbounding
heart of hearts.
The heart is all aquiver still … this late
and ever it fibrillates,
stayed, stayed, ennothinged,
unsparked in its obumbrous place,
belaid where it grounded.

— *June 6, 1990, June 25, 1990, October 20, 2017*

Visitors

They drive, knowing the way,
into the quiet city of Tulocay.
Exit their cars
in slow stirs.
The horror
is gone. Sorrow
clings on.
Loving still,
they groom the grassplay,
emplace bouquets.
At length turn away.
Time is certain.
Today
is tomorrow.
There is a falter
in the walker here ...
a devolving
downstep
on the steep stairs earthen.

—*July 1, 1990*
Tulocay Cemetery, Napa, California

Human Roses

Sprung born, unfolded slowly—human roses—
We are blushed and limbed, none of us written long—
Beloved among our own whilst twice the flung
Star twinkle-blinks, a fetal planet tosses
One throe in deep placental space, a rite
To become. To exist is everything.
Being is godlit—its embodying
Fleet phantomry.
                        We are taken in the night,
Forever windblown, moonshone ever. And what
We were, what were we, is now where, now where,
Cosmos most flowing?—'tis the what we are not,
In the stars'night O nuclear room of All
Birthing, All Ends ... Ubiquity's quarksquall
screaming ... beyond the fair dear air of Here.

—August 5, 1990

October

October is looking over
Sersel's Berg, Sissaly Q,
the saffron-laughing hue,
Unseenland,
Ramble Over,
Inbetweenland.
The betweens of doings
and conjurings,
undoings,
dreams, beings, redos,
still trues.
The in between
September,
November,
between amber
and umber,
between Greenleaf
and Fallenleaf
and Ollen's legal brief
and the campfire ember
of what we remember.

— October 16, 2017

The Mort Fence

There is a battle going on
behind the property line fence,
just over there.
It is a kind of life-clinging affair.
Dear is this world.
Mort the mortgage company
owns that property now.
What do Mort and his profiteers
care about a battle on their property,
a lawfulish life-and-death impropriety?
They've heard of unniceties.
Certain muzzle velocities.
The scandalous visits
of vandalism.
They've read the glossary of animosities,
of robbery and atrocity.
They fear only paucity.
Is there a solvency?
Mort the mortgage companeer
is wearing his comported lumpy leer
somewhere down in the city,
not so near.
He scratches his chinny-chin-cheer.
He is thoughtful on plausibilities,
possibles, certain revolving solvencies.
We, however, are seers
how dear the world is, so alive and near us.

— *October 17, 2017*

Token of Esteem

Neighbor, you have been alive,
you have come this way and done no harm.
You are slower now, seated in the shade,
still caring for what you behold.
This, your accolade,
thanks you, for your careful stride,
your easy farm,
your absence of storm,
the kindness underlying.
We do come this way,
this walk of beings.
Perhaps undamaging.
Perhaps to soothe the crying.

— *October 18, 2017*

The Knell

I can hear the knell,
but do not know the bell.
There is a church bell,
but this is more a dirge knell.
From where? It peals
as though from the bottom of a well.
Or a mineshaft.
We have those, once fine, now daft.
All danger.
The knell is swelling.
What meaning rings it?
What song would sing this?
Something comes.
A hand of thumbs.
Mouths without tongues.
Minds with guns.
There is a growl tolling,
a bell's tongue echoing.

— *October 18, 2017*

A Certainty Went

A certain certainty went
by us, bye us,
went away down the Ortenty Vent,
a part of the Blueskull Canyon.
That certainty was three messiahs
to the people of Little Newskull,
there in the canyon.
The Little Newskullians
intended the true and the truesome.
They are now untried and abusive
and denied and inexcusable.
A certain faith went
past them, too fast for them,
and down it went
into the Ortenty Vent.
The Little Newskullians now
with minds enlightening
their thoughtways, throughways,
true and new Newskull ways,
must follow the dream of reconstruing,
must wake and take up
that which they have yet and have not lost,
did not lose when that which was a certainty went
by, past, too fast, last and bye
down the Ortenty Vent.

— October 20, 2017

Big Pharma, Big Farma, Little Arms

There is an ambulating bank in the world.
Phone it, go online and view it,
find its bigwalk bank flag unfurled,
waving power in the skyscraping air.
Look far down the valley, you can see it coming, going,
thumping the crops, all of them growing.
The same bank sells your meds.
Look at the asking prices. Scratch your heads
and your headaches.
Greenbacks, pounds, euros, the big bank
yanks them all. Pay up.
Little farmers, little arms,
little children charmers, we'll have you all.
Hope you can medicate when you fall.
Hope the med waters will dream of you.
Hope beyond hope there are no dead lakes.

— *October 21, 2017*

Sampan Sandusky

Down at the Lamp and
Offering, they called him Sampan,
after a former place and form of residence
that he couldn't quit talking about.
He told the stoppers-by and the coffee-ers
and the others at the Lamp and Offering
that he had camped on a sampan for eight years
and it brought him to a view of opposites.
Knowing there was an opposite of himself,
some toppleganger, he was no longer an asserter.
Before the sampan there had been Susan City,
two parents, grandparents, a brother,
a sister pick-choosy,
a deacon, two dozen instructors, and a citizenry
supposedly varied.
These had regarded opposites, when at all,
as separate entities unrelated;
one jumped on and one jumped off.
But both flew over the blue crew's nest
always, held the ball in rapturous balance,
coexisted, as it were, in delicate rapport,
overruled the laws of time and space
and occupied the same air at the same moment.
Why did it take a snapping of cultures
and a creaking sampan on the other side of the planet
to teach him about this simple force field,
consequential ballots, this elemental balance
that truly held all intercourse in sway?

— *1970s, 2017*

209

Murgatroid Millwilliker

A fulltime parttime census-taker, he,
who came at length to ask what it was
men so curiously counted all their lives,
and why, and whereto.
Life as a series of objects? No. What was all the buzz?
He needed a little less of the work he needed.
His father had reared him in a bakery,
so he transferred to take the census
in the Whitefire Desert.
He ran out of engine at Blindout, population zero,
and out of water about thirteen miles from Filthy Rock
where Drygulch Amos Wrandy had always (it seemed)
resided as "one half" on the county census.
Murgie made ten of the thirteen miles and collapsed
and Drygulch Amos, perhaps in his usual periabout
and true to the poem being written,
came upon him with water.

Now for the point poor Murgatroint would have me make.
A letter, desert-caked, managed to arrive
at the Burnt Bush County hotseat
addressed to the recorder
of the ultracompulsory numericals of order
of the Burnt Bush County census, to wit:

Dear Sirs:
I Murgatroid Millwilliker *am still alive*
and do possess yet a functional mind
which has arrived at the following conclusion:
Life can perhaps be measured or expressed
like love or melted snow or bloodpressure
but counting it is a census-taker's errand,
it results in a thirsty unconscious contusion.
However, having been hired to do a job
out and about at every doorknob

I realize you require a *number*
instead of an emotion or a weight or a wonder.
Since I do not intend to return
please note the following report of population
in the Whitefire Desert:
At Flat Gorge, George and Millie Pillforge, 2.
At Burnished Bitch, Cyrus Hymus, 1.
At Coldcactus Cutoff, zero.
At Slanky Wash, Slanky Washburn, 1.
At Rosewither Wallow, Sweet Heather Brandywine
    and Rotfoot Forkins, 2.
At Blindout and at Crispy Croak, zero.
At Whatwater Nowhere, Snakeeye Halfway, 1.
And at Filthy Rock, Drygulch Amos Wrandy
and all the universe.

         — *1970s, 2017*

Reticles

There are the finest lines in your optical devices.
Open your opticals. Are you seeing.
There are the finest demarkations in the determinings
along your brainways, and sparkles leap your synapses.
Be cautious of curdlings, you want clarity
in what your map sees.
Open your inner opticals. Are you seeing.
Scope it out, I tell you. Distrust your lapses.
Scope it out, I tell you. All those perhapses.

— *October 25, 2017*

Gashrahm Gami

Gashrahm Gami in his ashram there
in Loggowottomy
learned to stare
from the vale of tears
blinkless, endless into anywhere
and after a hundred years
of glare
anywhere was everywhere.

— *1970s, 2017*

The Hoppowotomus

In certain circles it is a given
that you cannot catch a hoppowotomus.
In other circles it is, "A hoppo*what*omus?"
But in certain circles it is a head-scratching given
that it is easier to catch a cheetingtah, a charging whah,
a dizmoreemus or a ratcheting gibbon
than a hippity-hopalong hoppowotomus.
It has never been proven to the satisfaction
of the proofseekers that the hoppowotomus exists.
If the 'what'mus existed it would have a license,
says science, the sighing ice of science.
But in certain circles the proof is the say-so
of Idjapreem Othern. You see, Idjapreem
has tried everything. He is an acknowledged expert
at this task that cannot be accomplished.
He also conveys his error-laden terror
of the hoppowotomus. To his circle he asserts
that a hoppowotomus is part northpolecat,
part sprangarang, parts tuskerlope,
bearoxamus, hillierbeest, aurora boar.
And on the northern slope
should you encounter a 'what'mus, it hurts.
The 'what'mus does not exist,
the hurts they do persist.

— October 25, 2017

Rayder Gramble and the Songstress

Rayder Gramble fell in love, pray or tell,
with a songstress from Tuscarumbia
who made it big in the posh hotels,
and couldn't see her way toward yielding up
for the mere love of one
the larger love of the many.

No one peered into the well
(save Rayder) to see the rather keen distinction
between the loves, the love for the performer
and the love for the warmer.

Wherever she trilled
was her one Rayder Gramble, stilled
and patient in silent love's attendance.
He waited while she rang the bells.

People don't live long.
A life viewed in retrospect
seems but a moment,
a flicker of recognition,
a glimpse of the dawn
one with the sunset.
Perhaps that is why
the next thing she knew
he was one to her who felt in deepnesses
and loved her. Was there some sweetness
in her, could he know?
Who of the many would ever love her
apart from the love for the bird in her throat?

The change in her jeweled vowels,
a change for the eventual,
took hold the night she played
the crowded Misty Cabana
and rang her loudest bells.
She was taking her final bow
when she espied him walking intently
through a sea of hands
toward the stage,

an unreality he
in the neon-red sea.
She watched in disbelief
as he set a flower on the stage
and walked his placid passion out.

So there she stood
between the public present
and the coupled future
staring at that flower. It doesn't look real
she thought. Pick it up
she thought. She picked it up.
Its feel was real.
She bowed again
and made her exit.

In the neon-red air
she had taken the chrysanthemum
for pink and paper, a pulpanthemum.
Backstage it looked yellow
but its feel was real. She sniffed it—
no fragrance, but an efflux
of earthmusk.
Who of the many would ever love her
apart from loving the thrush in her throat?
She neared the door to the world outside,
real and more real came the white chrysanthemum,
until she stood in the wind and sun
holding a flower of the living earth.
Only back in there
in the neon-dark air
had Nature been unreal
and Love unfair.

— 1970s, 2017

Lee Kum Too

Lee Kum came to America
(no lesser place) on stowamariner
status of his own stealth,
to begin anew after incurring the ill health
of official governmental disfavor
in the homeland. He had claimed the land
was not the home. Nor was the home the land.
When Lee Kum Too
disembarked with eighty others,
sisters and brothers,
America asked why he had come too.
He told America that was his name and he had had to come.
And he asked in return
questions about rights human and civil
and his eyes were suns of incredulity
when America said, "Those are privileges,
not rights." Do the villages
believe this? was a spillage
forth from Lee Kum Too.
He said he could have heard that in the homeland;
what in hell was happening to America?
America thought for a moment and did not answer,
but admitted Lee Kum Too unto the tried and true
through its pearly Golden Gate in silence—
in which land (no less than legally adopted as his own)
Lee Kum Too is spreading the word: "I came to
when man became too heavy
with too much hatred in my homeland;
and I came too
to say Beware.
Beware and beware again.
Beware of all the angers Love is not
and all the walls Freedom is not."
Lee Kum Too came too
and is spreading the word:
the absolution of the hatreds
and the gentle reattuning of the greeds.
And Beware all worlds
of the fall of Freedom.

— 1970s, 2017

Twelve token poems,

love-broken crumbs

Nine sonnets, three freeform poems, originating in the 1970s.

Were I Vying in a Vale of Tears

If you were dwelling in a swell of time
And I were vying in a vale of tears;
If you were moonful in a bloom of mime
And I were caroling a fable of fears;
If you took slumber in a reverie
And I took waking in a vigil of rain;
If you took giving for your company
And I consorted in the vain membrane;
Still were I set to find you, still were I
Intent upon my own redemption: You.
Yet one were we to walk a star to sky
And new was I to know my loving true.
You were the whole, therefore I was entire
Should my part burn upon the merciful pyre.

Were We One

If we were two and our love one, what wind
Could stir the calm of us? Recall the dove,
However, that our one calm brought in to mend:
We warmed it, nursed it, thought we imparted love
But we imparted air and liberty,
The sky above the health within the wing.
We gave again the nature to be free;
The love returned was spirit wandering.
And it was wandered, and at once I knew
Nothing at all about that bird and what
A bird might be, or mean. But I mean You.
And I mean That Between Us which is not.
And now I mean as well it never was
If it can end within the both of us.

There Comes Assured and Bright

So if I love you will I bear your joy
A little while forever, lovingness,
And I will hide you from my sober ploy!
There comes no harm, no nightfall, poetess!
There comes, assured and bright, what muse you fancy,
What way you journey, and what song you sing.
Now stand, glow, shrug away halt hesitancy,
Step forward, amble, bring what you will bring.
Your tortoise lumbers with you, though he wear
His static sanctum yet—within whose walls
He writhes, a titan, toward the brilliant air,
Grasps it, gasps it, and captive still he crawls.
So do I love you. Let us find the spring
Not by my fastness, but by your swift wing.

A Separate Ecstasy

Now that your gleaming eyes are dark in dream,
And all the flowers of your entity
Huddling in desire of dawn; and we,
The substances of our devoted scheme
Of intimate commerce, the delighted team
Of misfits, have denounced ability
Favoring renewal: now I seek in me
A separate ecstasy. And if I seem
Far off from our unasking idleness,
Remember that I go in search of this:
My self, the now renewed. That I love you
Doubt not. That I am of you, doubt you less.
I go because the agony is bliss
That renders Prior an enamored True.

Never Hand You Up

So shall I never hand you up to Death,
Whose flaxen fingers furled about the knife
Unhinge the lung from its affair with breath,
Bisect the nettled need apart from Life,
Make separate members of the seed and leaf.
And never shall I see you into Winter,
Whose frigid finger freezes from the eave
To point the haven where the heart shall enter
With all its consorts, all its loves and art,
Never to rise again in form of heart.
Stone shall lie jewel when all wings depart,
The earth is tranquil every tempest knows.
So shall you never in the blow that snows
Be handed out; let snow hand up a rose.

There Sees One Eye

In all there is, in turning and in Time
There sees one single eye; in all of life
There shines one solitary knowing-clime;
For all of this absurdity and strife
There is one weather and a single hour
Sufficient and conducive to the cause
Of seeing—in harmony with the mull contour
Of knowing: there is one sunlight and one pause
Given to the perfect circumstance of growth.
And in that hour one is beauteous
With knowing and knowing nothing, with the both.
And knowing and nothing are all-bounteous,
And one grows forward into loving what
He must become before his love is not.

Winteredness Flower

Since left in winteredness and desolate
Despair, my thoughts would save their mind, so turn
To you, and I to tell you this now burn
A midnight lamp; I scrawl a word, debate,
Delete, rewrite the word, obliterate
The thought, begin again. I would you learn
The narrow inward straits I navigate
Vanished, adrift, so harrowed, so unsound
I clearly but your flowers can discern,
Urged burgeons both on tabletops arrayed
And through a lovely life arranged and wound.
You carry inner flowerets never spent,
Assuage a feverous brow with their rich aid,
And lay the battlefield to sleep unrent.

— 1970s, 2017

The Eye in All

And had I known I breathe the breath you breathe,
Then had I breathed again, and then believed,
And then come humbly forward to enwreathe
Our morning's vapor in a song retrieved.
And had I known I see the eye you see
In all there is, in worlds awhorl and Time,
And see the anguish in the felony
And the oldest slumber in the present mime;
And had I known that total plumbing eye
Had fathered ours alike, mine, yours, theirs, heirs,
All, and it was an eye in flight, all sky,
An eye beknownst the clouds amongst, the airs
Within, the winds. Believe that it beholds,
The all-Eye, futures, pasts, such news, such olds.

— 1970s, 2017

Flesh Child

Flesh is a child for harboring and pity,
For bringing to the fireside from the storm,
For feeding and protecting from alarm.
I have beheld the shoulder that is mighty.
Consider how the might has been a child
And never slackened from the childlike way.
What has become of morning at midday?
What mountain dams the blood the vein knew wild?
Blood is a rage that scowls and goes to sea
And wrings indignity from solid rock,
A scorn that makes a jollity of hurt
And stabs itself crusading to be free—
And labors piling block on top of block
That its tides pour in peace their rampant art.

Of War and Horn

I have heard a war horn
sounding some strange glory
in the night, as the bleeding story
dies.
Perhaps there shall be reseeding.
I have heard the speeches insistent and awry,
blaring hatred, outcry,
pain, scorn.
Then ply the war horns and extinction.
Cognition's flower can emblazon
yon dump of rubble in its foulest hour
with noble texture,
with yon dump's own dawn in its deepest rubble.
Though the burning horn,
yonder and imponderable,
aspires to summon silence with loud treason.

— late 1960s or early 1970s (as sonnet), rewritten 2017

Love's Own

Love is its own exquisite place.
Love's other face
Shows through window lace.
The other side of what I am
I know and feel but do not see,
It is the stealth and underneath of me.
The other side of beef is grief,
And the other sigh
Of potato's whispering blue sky
Seeps into the ear
And blue blurs the eye
Of the furtherese leper.
And the upper side
Of the underside of ground
Gleams with what I see in you,
With how I look upon your face.
This typewriter, a machine,
Metallic and mechanical,
Electric and eclacktic,
Bludgeons back to pulp
The paper white and pure
Whereon your sculpture
Somehow is, brow and fair;
Thums the paper white and pure
To sing of love,
A dream in air.

— 1970s, 2017

224

Lovegoing

I know that love
turns out its eye,
smiles and walks away.

I know that love
is going and must go.
Snow is decay.

I feel it going
and there is nothing to say.
The spring will come.

Love will dismount
from its celestial crystal.
Love will melt away.

Franklin Flood Falterlater

Franklin was a crisis intervention expert,
he stood like a seawall against the flood
of suicide, homicide, mayhem and hatred and hurt.
He came to be called an expert
by being credited with saving
over a thousand lives, stanching the flood of blood
on the telephone, over radio,
on the ledges of skyscrapers,
on the buttresstops of bridges.
And the living backed away from edges,
the living went on living.
When came his own crisis, however, a misgiving
of falling belief, a rusting mistrust of philosophy,
he proved to be one of a very few contrarians,
in his preeminent humanitarian career,
who saw the emotional meaninglessness
of his most persuasive and therapeutic
paragraphs, the glitters of his bookshelf,
paragraphs on survival through thick
and thinnest, on the sweet redemption of the self.

Someone Believes

There is a someone who believes a democracy
inferior to a numbing hard-knockracy.
A hard throw at a woman,
a swinging of the club.
And the someone knows
other someones.
How is it done, you wonder.
You first speak hatred in Milliwarne's garage.
Milliwarne hates the world.
If you nod your head, if your face agrees,
eventually you see the guns.
Guns will rule, Milliwarne avows.
We'll have a gunning tomorrow, not what now is.
Comes a militarious array of urns.
A martiocracy. A militocracy.

There is another someone, a someone else,
who believes a democracy
is echoing on the hill.
Below the hill, the people are passing,
as is their daily way,
but they listen if they will.

— November 2, 2017

Brampton Slambop Hampton

Slambop was a prizefighter
who, heavier or lighter,

never made it to the prize kablooeyous
because he lost his faith
in his particular pursuance.

He was fighting Barswell in a swift
ten-rounder on the way to the championship,
he landed an anvil of a handful
of a cruel right cross
to Barswell's protruding mandible
in the fifth.

Who's loss?

He watched Barswell's lolly-crossing eyes
and Barswell's dangling mandible
and Barswell's Barswell slumping into slumbering
and suddenly Barswell hit him back with pity.

It came in the form of an arcking roundhouse
to the tired mind's very entity
and Hampton, Hampton broke the ropes
departing that enclosure of interrupted hopes

and abrupt compassion
for all perpetuation.

— 1972

Umble the Hunchback

Umble was born hump first
and born to lean over
and walk like an ape.
But the apes were all those
who ever stood aside
and aped him and laughed him.
Umble was first to admit
he wasn't much.
He couldn't badmint,
could not pfut ball.
He wasn't handsome, part or all,
so ventured forth without a squeezieheart.
His only work was somewhere down under.
And at times he was first to admit
Death would be welcome if it came.
But how many truths are there?
Umble could see the world
from a place of his own,
and his place was unique.
He smiled at everyone and he could see
who smiled back, whether everyone or no one.
You could tell a smile from a smile from underneath.
But he didn't mind those smiles that weren't meant.
Umble could smile back at a smile unmeant
with a smile intent.
The only smile he minded was the wan smile
of pity. He saw that smile often, "the one smile,"
he called it, coughing.
People act differently,
for better or for worse,
when they see someone with less
than they have, when they thought they had little.
But a truth will follow a truth.
Umble's greatest desire
was to be a man

and love a woman.
Long ago he'd given up the bed.
It wasn't coming to him.
But once or twice a year
a woman would smile at him
without that awful pity.
It was then he was a man
and loved a woman.
And once he was even kissed
without that awful pity.
How tall had he been then,
and how straight,
and how proud?
And she had won
a lover in darkness
for as long as love would be.

— 1970s, 2017

Hazel Remembered

Your father fought fire
and died a smoke death.
Today
I see that smoke
in the fogbank from the crying coast.
And I see your freckled face
in that forever mist.

— 1970s, referencing a memory from about 1953

Syria, 2017

Humanity has a human right,
in a human world, to human life.
Would a demon rise otherwise
screaming demise?
Would an army of roaches
thunder near, umbrous encroachers
on the wondrous and the dear,
and that army fire on a non-army
there, somewhere, near?
In Syria the White Helmets come
to save lives. Heroic men, strong and gentle,
saviors of humanity.
Caring women come,
hoping they will not weep,
broken and atremble
in the murderdust.
"To save a life is to save all of humanity."
They come, they too fall into dying
in their perspiring prying
at rubbles outcrying,
they too in their noble trying.

— November 3, 2017

A Nonquote: If You've Seen One Redwood,
You've Seen 'Em All

I've sweated up Sweat Leg Ridge
and all its cave-age acreage
for half a day, half out of my way,
but out of old habit
I find the cabin.
Though McCumber's seventy-four or eighty-four or eight more
there's a young woman there, she charges nude
out the parched hewn door
and heaves a washbowl of water in my face.
"Oh! I'm sorry! I didn't see you," she says with haste.
"That's perfectly all wet, I needed it," are my replies.
"I've come to see Lumberbug McCumber,"
I inform her. "Is he nearabouts?"
"Don't know his hairy whereabouts,"
she blurps, follows my eyes,
remembers she is nude, and bounces inside,
calling back, "He went down toward Scare-a-Trout Creek
or thereabouts. I expect him back
sometime this week."
McCumber jumps out from his woodsy wonders,
spies me and cries, "Aha, you show-late
poet lowrate you!"
                            The greeting stage
consumes an hour and a supper.
"McCumber, old lumberer,
here's why I've humped up here.
A coat'n'tie below has throated and been quoted
when no lone groping soul should have noticed.
More or less, said he's seen the redwoods ... nothing beautiful ...
just upstood wood ... a little up-tall taller is all.
O apex-homèd sapient,
what can you say on it?"
He snorks, winks, strikes up his pipe,
inhaws a draw, claws his jaw.

"That's what he said, said he?
Sounds like droppings from a dead-word tree.
Well, I've been up here fifty years.
They've been fifty to the good.
I've come to know who's in the woods.
I'll chance to chat in behalf of half
of them at least, and probably most
of the other half alsost.
What can I say on it?
In the wild-eyed society
of naturalists, naturists, satyrs,
mountain men, earthylings, civilization-haters,
river rats, packers back, meditators,
prospectors, lost specters, rangers,
strangers, logmen, frogmen, foresters,
poor nesters, fishermen, aborigines, set-arounds,
primevalists, lakeladies, shade maidens, *et cetera*—
in this free-spirited and brush-eyed society
to make such a statement as your poem's entitlety
is a plain and immediate impiety.
Whoever said it cannot eye a tree.
And you can tell him for me,
whoever he be,
that I'd not want to trust him with the fate
of the lofty, the growing, or the great of weight."

—1980s

Panthony Pools

Pools was born in one. They called it a first
(it wasn't) and gave it a name: wetbirth
(it was). Panthony found the swimming rough.
The ancient labor of birth would have been amazement
enough, but truly the labor of the nascence of Panthony
was his flipsquid father Scranthony
kneeling at the pool's edge
tilting at his mother's head with a mallet.
But Panthony despite his drenched misgiving
made it to living, to life as they call it.
His mother hauled him up by the cord
and threw him at his father
and when the power and the progeny abruptly met
Panthony drew the abrupted breath.

All of his unmade maiden-sister
life-laden auntie spinsters
feared the effect of the water, they said with winces,
but feared in secret fact the effect
of irregular circumstance on the orb atop his neck.
"He'll be a waterbaby, no doubt, no maybe,
and his brain will float about, no maybe, no doubt."

But Panthony Pools had thought to swim
before he had learned to breathe and live;
he was indeed a child where the waters are.
His head, however, proved a shine over fine—
thoughtful with its innate intimate star
and boxcar-ajar to all the stars there are.

                              — *original draft 1970s*

Sutherland Springs

Today Death came, a Baptist-tapping,
an inane disdaining ignorance
of the ship of worship,
of the pith of faith,
the zombie finger, an indentured fervent,
triggering away in the perverse curl of ignorance,
in the horrid conqueruity
slaying the prayersayers.
Comes on a dampening of the thumping of hearts.
Where would the nit of wit flit now
but down the road to yet another
wheeled billet of bullets,
and yet another passing,
then the stillness, a Texas whisper.
Back at the church, the impained
and the lurching,
the anguished,
a consolation prayer crying,
a crawl, sprawl, a nothing at all,
a one moan,
the gone on.

— November 5, 2017

Fats Holyoak

The holy oak of endurance and girth
found an oak's birth
out of an acorn and earth
back when peace and growing were a worth.
Oaken Fats learned long days of sunlight
aglimmer throughout him.
And long nights of rain
adrip from him.
He was Pax Holyoak.
Then they brought him a war.
He waved a leaf and went on growing.
Then they tried to induct him
but his roots were deep in the conduction
of sustenance from the wellspring,
each root a health string,
and he went on believing.
Reluctantly they fired on him in anger
with awfulmatic rifles,
which brought about a scarred demeanor
but failed to penetrate to the true believer.
In a mounting frustration that a tree
meant more to a tree than a war,
they grenaded him.
In response he serenaded with a limb
thin as a twig and grew ahead.
In response to the twig the ever-at-warriors
brought up a rocket-launcher and launched,
and Fats took a massive puncture in the trunk.
In response he waved and believed.
In response to the wave and belief
they fired a recoilless rifle,
Fats grawled an awful stifle
and grew.
In response to the persistery
they called in artillery.

He coughed. He believed.
Then the metal eagles
old Fats
droned overhead
and the fivehundreds fell,
after them the thousanders,
after them the trunkbusters,
and Fats did stand, unjusted,
stunted a mite, perhaps,
but implanted still
in the deep earth of faith.
But now
old Fats
a single condor
swollen with a single egg of centers
has taken the sky,
the wound of its thrown eggstorm
breaking the bones life meant to form
and silencing the cry life would have heard
will be half your known earth:
O what of belief now,
Fats,
old Fats,
will you now, the final moment,
drink with love in the root-tip yet
from the infinite fountain of life,
and believe it blessed?

— 1972; November 6, 2017

Wizenry

My old friend claims to be wizened.
Is he is or is he isn't?
He has oldened the tenfolds
since he was ten of old.
So much is so. He has sold
some youth,
in that there is some truth.
But is he long in the tooth?
I remember him in the California
diurnal aurora,
tenfolds ago.
Wizardry, no wizenations.
Time reaches out
for the periodic, the episodic, the epoch,
touches unseen the seasons
through instants, minutes,
hours, flowers,
some mystic in it,
somehow it is infinite.
The clocks are rhythmic,
complex with whiles,
the instances are guiles.
The clocks they fathom nothing
of the unknown something.

— for Scott, November 7, 2017

The Thirteenth Month

My calendar has a thirteenth month, Truvember.
What can it mean? Something somehow true
in a flied and flown untruth?
Something yet heartwarm in an ember
drooling cool?
Something somehow gone but true
in the lost remembering in you?
From whence came this departure
from the calendar long known, the heartsure?
Would November, of a sudden, traverse
an unknown era source,
a darkling arc of Truvember,
to arrive at December,
the known, the long known, the trusted,
the decent remembered
of the year undusted?

— *November 16, 2017*

Kilpatrick Filnaddrick McPatrick, Industrial Spy

Kilpat lived handsomely awhile
photographing contracts, blueprints, documents,
thoughtwhacks, buybacks, abstracts,
and extracting high secrets via psychological wrack
from opposition executive supposition.
Then, then came the order to become the purloiner of the toolkit
of the human esthetic, years, years prior to exquisite fulfillment,
so that a demand might be studiously cultivated
in the supplicating consumer public for a suitable duplicate.
Kilpatrick and unhappiness.
Then, then came the order to facelift the human philosophic
years in advance of the peace it might have made,
so that a demand might be painstakingly created
in the perambulating purse-string public
for an apathetic compress and an ethic of total commerce,
both to be manufactured by the home corporation.
Kilpatrick and despair. Worse had become worse.
Then, then came the order to kill.
Kilpatrick refused frenetic on a cumulous rug
with an emetic accumulation of refusals,
tucked his severance pay into his shoe,
and fled away at an elegiac amble:
after which amnesic meanderation
he discovered himself in an overturned boxcar
in the scars along the yards with a determined libertine
called Freddy the Freight Weevil.
In whose most sympathetic
and self-suspended company
Kilpatrick departed the megalopolitan mountains
and the wretched loveless smiling
nonhearted corporate brass brains forever.

— 1972, 2017

The Incredible Warningbell of Hankford Sawsbury Peoria

Hankford's family, once of Sawsbury, then of Peoria, were townies.
What is in a name? Oh, this and that, upsies and downies.
A bell rang deep within the disturbance in baby Hankford's
unconsciousness at his expulsion from uteral bliss.
It rang again ere the hazards of boyhood drew blood.
Then it began to ring before risk was visible, danger discernible.
They wondered how he went about preknowing.
Then the bell rang out in swell the day before an act of hatred
tore Europe free of its frustration
and imprisoned it in anger.
It rang again behind the moon the night before Hankford learned
his nation was intervening
in the chaos careening.
It rang the day his brother, screaming
Hank and Hank, died convulsive in that Great Wrath.
And it would ring the night before
his nation landed troops in any other nation's cry of war
to patrol the revolutions of the oppressed and the sore.
Though the others were listening, listening to foretell,
Hank alone could hear the bell, ringing in the Hankford Citadel.
It rang before the vast pecuniary lunacy,
the depression into badwater where so many drank.
An incredible bell indeed, it tolled imperative late in the night
of December 6, 1941 and woke him out of Oregon
before the wide windy Pacific in which life, in some form,
must, must urgently, must have been being born.
But he knew, in a certain Pacific silver and a sky in blue,
that life being born had not awakened him.
Life about to be taken, life about to end had awakened him.
Hankford tried to phone a warning,
no one would be warned by Hankford's knell.
That bell tolled again one minute before December 8, 1941
so help him god.
And then it almost blew his head apart twice
during August of 1945 immediately prior

to all hell and fire.
It pealed for Korea and Indochina and Suez and Cuba.
It clanged before assassinations
and again for Indochina and again for Suez,
and for the pierced hearts of nations.
Hankford tells me he's having bellsy headaches.
He tells he feels
the bell's about to peal again
and peal for real.
He says that soon, in terms of lifetimes,
times will loom rife
with anguish and with strife,
and Hankford's bell will ring out in the ears of all men
simultaneously and at once, in an all when
of crises, as though all men
were of one mind.

— 1972, 2017

The What Where

Upon some hour, in the slow locales of days,
might your care and search declare
you have arrived at last in the hard-sought where,
though you tip-and-toe
and heel-and-toe-and-fro still,
pondering why you recognize
search's end not,
whereas is where,
and all of here is what?

— November 17, 2017

Bernabino Binby

Bernie spent half his life on a farm
and the other half in a casino.
The farm yielded crops
and the brightnight neons of the gambling lake
a risk at the nerve ends, perhaps or perhaps not a take.
And these were Binby's questions:
How beautiful was the land,
the land that feeds, the land awake?
It gave him a harvest twice in the year of seasons,
in a land's way and with soil's reasons.
It had given him a home and would become his home.
It gave him constancy.
And how beautiful was a roll of the dice—
the outcome unknown and unredoable,
all to be won, all to be lost, flowers or ice.
And Bernie spent half his life on a farm
and Bernabino the other half in a casino.
Each man was Bernie but which man was Binby?
He asked and did not know.
Bernie knew both men and did not know either.
The question ached within him with such dubiety
that he elected to settle the riddle and ask society.
Now they hold bimonthly
Gamblers Agronomous meetings
at the Binby farm.
And the omnidirectional mind
cycles in circles like a whirlwind,
telling bluntly
all that it sees.

— 1970s, 2017

243

The Bonemarrow Chronicle of QuickSioux Howley

Jigtrue Howley, born into Carolina in 1862,
became at the age of one moment a howler in protest of rebirth,
it pained him so. He cried for six months
and moaned for a year.
Carolina knew it had a special son when at age three years
he said he had foreseen defeat and surrender. All was unwon,
yet a future of life and living was to be done.
They called him a man when he was nine
and he left Carolina for a westward of the mind.
Big wind, buffalo, but there were wars with Indians.
Fool that the West proclaimed him he wouldn't fight.
He rode to the Sioux under a banner serene and white.
He met a toothless elder fine of shelter.
Howley promised he was not a murderer.
A few Lakota laughed at him, yet they thought him true.
Howley came away, white-flag Jigtrue and slightly Sioux.

High in Montana Howley fired on a bear that wasn't.
A kind of quiet was the bear's gaze. In the echo of that shot
stood Howley in a freeze of fear like time taken root.
Had he lost a truth? What kind of must-not had he wrought?
He had failed to love life more than he feared it.

Six years after he had departed it he returned alone
through Lakota lands, seeking the heart of it. The Indians were fewer
and a winter wind blew in their faces though it was spring.
Howley found a knowing of years oncoming,
and within him that long-forgotten moan set in.
He sang his plainsong and took his leave of the plainsmen.

Back in the Carolina of his long befores
Howley heard word of dying and of wars
in places he knew not, and the earth of Carolina sad was sighing.

While Howley rocked away on a Carolina veranda
chanting to himself a song of the sun and plains and Montana
and the mountain fountains
he learned of the massacre of the exhausted
and draining Miniconjou blood at Wounded Knee
so quickly frosted.
No longer free.

Howley moaned that early moan again in his breast.
He stood and spread his arms wide to the one sun
and screamed, "Life is to Be,
not to die, not die, but to Be! Be!"
He had learned to love Life as it might be loved.
And Life could hear that moan in his breast.

Someone called his name for San Juan Hill
but fool that he was, wasn't he, he wouldn't kill.
And he had breast to moan again
the many thousands at the thoughtless Marne,
trenchwar, wrench of death, hatred's burn and scarring.
And to moan again the failure to pool our separate peaces
into one League and one dream.

When Howley died in Carolina in 1940
he died moaning that original moan,
and his last word was a curse for the faith of guns,
a faith we would return to.
His few friends at the burial site were taken aback
when a tall red man appeared among them
and stood quietly with bowed head, and went away again.
Now it so happened they planted Howley
under an ancient oak, grumbly and growly
in storm and stormsoak.
Three weeks after he assumed his ground
a hurricane plucked up
oak tree and and roots and Howley, all.
They found him stood on end
and the coffin lid flown off with wind
and his right eye reopened on Carolina.
Nations were falling
and he moaned in there
like a wind in a cavern.
Old Tom Two Elks the inebriate halfbreed from Ouchy's Tavern
pulled a note and pencil
from Howley's green hand:
"Life is not to die and to die and to die
but forever to Be and to Be and to Be."

— *1970s, 2017*

245

Ticket Ackerman

Ackerman was ticketed a ticket a month
for running a red flashing traffic light
at a quarter of six in the morning, ticket after ticket
at the same intersection, dashing
in disdain through the redness flashing
at Finewine Boulevard and Apple Cider Avenue.
With every ticket Officer Fraygray proclaimed,
"This citation could save your life";
and Ackerman replied for the sake of strife,
"This citation could save your station."
On the first of the month they were laying for him—
Felix Fraygray and Samuel Sawlsbarry,
minions of the presbytery.
The first of the month was Ackerman Day.
On the tenth consecutive first of the month
Ackerman beckoned in the ticket
that brought him snickering
before Municipal Court Traffic Division Judge
Bernard B. Bracy, who issued a tissue of municipal admonition.
And the first went on being Ackerman Day.
On the eighteenth consecutive first of the month
Ackerman laughing with more than his mouth
spied the patrol car coined for collection
and drove through red at four miles an hour,
which drew him his eighteenth citation.
Fraygray shook his head and asked,
"After slowing down so much
why didn't you just stop for once?"
Ackerman replied with a crooked wince,
"You didn't see that light flash 'walk'?
I thought maybe you wouldn't write me up
and we could skip our little talk
if I went through the walk light *at a walk*."
"Very funny, Ackerman," Fraygray retorted.
"Why don't you try smart and unreported?"
And Ackerman went once more becourted
before Municipal Court Traffic Division
Judge Bernard B. Bracy, who asked in a patriarchal drawl,
"Why must you persist, Mister ... uh ... Ackerman,
in running this particular vehicular restriculor,

in direct defiance and annoyant destroyance
of a perfectly good and valid statute
hashed about and scratched out
for the plentiful wellbeing and general safeseeing
of men, women, children and statues
as well as for you the highwayman?"
Ackerman replied in a patriarchal drawl
and Bracy suspended his license.
The following Ticket Ackerman Day,
habit had Fraygray and Sawlsbarry parked like a spider
at the crossing of Finewine and hard Apple Cider,
Ackerman came off the hill on a bicycle
and tore through the scarlet glower
at fifty miles an hour.
It was six city blocks
before they could pull him over.
Samuel Sawlsbarry read him his knocks,
and Ackerman appeared in the violation docks
before Municipal Court Traffic Division
Judge Bernard B. Bracy, who suspended his cyclense.
The following first of the month at a certain intersection
at five-forty-five in the dawning glint
Fraygray and Sawlsbarry were parked content
and half-asleep in an Ackerman squint,
Ackerman faithful to his insurrection
came off the hill at a footlong sprint
and tore through the don't-walk light
at twenty miles an hour.
Sawlsbarry wrote him a ticket for jayrunning.
And Ackerman went playfunning
before Municipal Court Traffic Division
Judge Bernard B. Bracy, who suspended his runcense
and fined him a hundred bills or a hundred days.
Ackerman took the hundred days.
An officer led him to another officer
who led him to another officer
who sashayed him to the calaboose.
An officer at the calaboose
held out his hand and asked, "Where's the ticket?"
The officer with Ackerman replied,
"What ticket?" The calaboosifer shrugged and sighed,
"I can't take him without a ticket."

He looked at Ackerman. "Where's the ticket?"
Ackerman answered, "Sawlsbarry has it."
Sixty days later
Ackerman was coming out
on good behavior to the letter;
the turnkey asked in a wristabout,
"You got a ticket?"
Ackerman said, "What for? Is there a show?"
The turnkey replied, "It's *all* a show,"
and turned the key,
"and no one's admitted free.
You have to have a ticket.
It starts when you're born.
They write a ticket that says you're born,
here is your ticket. Lose your ticket
and you've mispreserved your verve."
The following day was the first of the month.
Ackerman came over the hill
and through the intersection
in a gyrocopter a foot off the ground.
Fraygray wrote him a ticket for gyronautical obstruction
and misuse of the roadways, for disregarding The Oughticles
of Roadicol, and for gyrating under the impudence.
And Ackerman took his impish nuisance
before Municipal Court Traffic Division
Judge Bernard B. Bracy, who suspended his gyrence
and fined him a hundred bills or a hundred days.
Ackerman took the hundred days.
Sixty days later Ackerman came out
on good behavior, sixty counts,
and sat down in a parking space
in the street next to the curb.
In three minutes' grace
a madman in a chevrolac
was honking the horn to detune and wrack
but Ackerman wouldn't move his face.
He had his rights and wrongs whatever they were
and no one could tell him they weren't his own, loud sir.
Fraygray wrote a ticket
for occultophysical obstruction of the parking ways
and stuffed it in Ackerman's pocket maze.
And Ackerman took his disputant daze

before Municipal Court Traffic Division
Judge Bernard B. Bracy, who suspended his sitcense
and sentenced him to a hundred days.
Sixty days later Ackerman came out with a certain bounce
on good behavior, sixty counts,
and rode a horse by the name of Ambrose
into the capitol session chamber
where the lip-and-waity legislature
might have been swayed to remember
that clemency is vaster than shame-uponcy.
Ambrose was of a lake opinion.
Sawlsbarry wrote them a ticket
for bursting innards and horselature.
And Ackerman went before
Municipal Court Criminal Division
Judge Bernard B. Bracy,
who suspended his horsesense
and sentenced him to another hundred ways, you see.

— 1970s, 2017

Terrorsode

The thing happened. There was a kind of nonthinking
variant vile veering from what might be thought
right, the right we achieved by struggling a hard path
and arriving wounded, worn, torn, but our sons thinking.
And our daughters knowing.
And a thing happened. And wrong came, bought
by riches hidden away in dungeons and caves.
And to hold in hand the riches, wrong came, loathing peppers
of speech and harm and untogethers.
And now, would the thing return?
We learn quiet guns are walking again in the fallen night,
peering, peering with the single eye of guns,
seeking the terrors in the hearts of ones
shrouded in shadow in hope of the morrow,
terrors praying that the nevers
are never, not evers,
never agains of horror,
that no abhorrent torpor
beset Son Wondering,
Lady Dream, Lady Love One,
until we are lost for him,
until we mourn her,
for no restoring of her.

— *November 29, 2017*

A Fourteenth

If there were a fourteenth and a She
and a gloried Her aurora beheld by
a certain other interior sight, by a seeing
of what is well and what belongs,
tell, what could it mean?
Could it mean that years would come golden?
That tenfolds gently would know the folding,
that rivers would flow in
sunlit river-pensive olden roiling,
in river-sung songs?
A She and a fourteenth,
in the worldlit morning
beholding, mooring,
pouring, deeming,
dreaming, adoring.

— for Helen, November 14, 2017

She Too

She remembers the desire that was uncaring.
A force overbearing,
caustic, like the burned hands of war.
She steps forward.
The response is blaring.
She is human.
Do not treat her otherwise,
netherwise,
subhumanwise,
less-than-womanwise,
less-than-herselfwise.
Perhaps it is true
that she is beautiful.
Truthful this:
Beautiful is human.
Beautiful is human is new and is woman
and is new man and is human
and caring is feasible.
Come to know it, you,
please.
You are you
and you are able.

— November 19, 2017

Singularities

There are, beyond us, at distances incomprehensible,
immeasurable densities,
the unexultant result of gravity
gone utter, to phenomenon, in tumult and darkness.
And there are, beyond us, in rampant majesty,
infinite nondensities,
weightless dancings of light beads in farness.
And hereabouts, there are indefinite propensities.
And in all wheres there is the profoundly indistinct:
instinct, the unlinked, the undepicted, the now extinct.
And in human wheres, wheres of whom and true cares,
there is the croon of the unique:
esteem, dreams beyond dreams, so-to-speaks, the mystique.
And in the sphere of reason, of cerebration of seemscape,
there is the thought, the thought out, the thinkabout,
the unthinkable as familiar
as the touch of one's hand,
as a willing listener,
as happening as a castle
blooming unmanned of its own,
a palace upasking
in the lasting sand.

— November 26, 2017

The Wherefore

There is a wherefore at the corner,
just beyond the why,
past the whereupon discarded.
We are obliged to go it on,
to dredge up the dripping whyfors,
think merlins, friars and cipherers,
to think it through and throughout.
Yes, it follows that we are new at
thrashabout, fallout, and the scout
for truth. But our genes are old at it.
We have been the ancient road before,
even long before the sword,
long enough before to make lore.
And we are still ourselves,
speakers by hours and twenties and twelves,
the makers of routes onward,
the thought ones,
the dancers in leaves,
the lanterners,
the answerers.

— *November 10, 2017*

The Tenfolds

Tenfolds are the decades, a tenfold each.
Ten oldings are a tenfold.
We have been told
five tenfolds past, that is gone olden
now, all olden.
But five tenfolds past, that is also
lone minutes now,
gone but gathered
torn storms on a human brow.
Loves in the eye dimmed, yet aglow.
Mere instants enfolded.
We knew those times once.
The tenfolds are not so gone, gone so olden.
True, they are marked away with clocks, with happenings,
with days, with driftings, with sleeps,
with the absconding falsehoods of calendars.

— *October 9, 2017*

www.ingramcontent.com/pod-product-compliance
Lightning Source LLC
Chambersburg PA
CBHW070951040426
42443CB00007B/466